Ending c ⸱ ⸱y for good

C000046462

Edited by Josephine Tucker

CPAG • 30 Micawber Street • London N1 7TB

Child Poverty Action Group works on behalf of the more than one in four children in the UK growing up in poverty. It does not have to be like this. We use our understanding of what causes poverty and the impact it has on children's lives to campaign for policies that will prevent and solve poverty – for good. We provide training, advice and information to make sure hard-up families get the financial support they need. We also carry out high-profile legal work to establish and protect families' rights. If you are not already supporting us, please consider making a donation, or ask for details of our membership schemes, training courses and publications.

Published by Child Poverty Action Group
30 Micawber Street
London N1 7TB
Tel: 020 7837 7979
staff@cpag.org.uk
www.cpag.org.uk

The views expressed are those of the authors and do not necessarily represent the views of the Child Poverty Action Group.

© Child Poverty Action Group 2020. Contains public sector information licensed under Open Government Licence v3.0.

A CIP record for this book is available from the British Library
ISBN: 978 1 910715 71 0

Child Poverty Action Group is a charity registered in England and Wales (registration number 294841) and in Scotland (registration number SC039339), and is a company limited by guarantee, registered in England (registration number 1993854). VAT number: 690 808117

Cover design by Colorido Studios
Cover illustration by sketchpadstudio.com
Typeset by Devious Designs
Printed in the UK by CPI Group (UK) Ltd

About the editor

Josephine Tucker is Head of Policy and Research at CPAG. Her role involves analysis of the causes, consequences and experience of poverty in the UK, and the promotion of effective policies to secure family incomes and reduce hardship facing children.

Acknowledgements

We are very grateful to everyone from the UK and New Zealand who has contributed so enthusiastically to this book. It is heartening to realise that so many experts and leaders are committed to ending child poverty. In addition we thank Jonathan Bradshaw for his valuable comments on draft chapters, Nicola Johnston for overseeing production, Sundus Pasha for very diligent editing and Kathleen Armstrong for proofreading.

About the authors

Rt Hon Jacinda Ardern is Prime Minister of New Zealand, Minister for Child Poverty Reduction.

Jonathan Bradshaw is Emeritus Professor of Social Policy at the University of York, and a member of the Policy Committee of Child Poverty Action Group.

Torsten Bell is the Chief Executive of the Resolution Foundation, an independent think tank focused on improving living standards for those on low to middle incomes.

Davara Bennett is a PhD student in the Department of Public Health and Policy at the University of Liverpool.

Fran Bennett is a Senior Research and Teaching Fellow at the Department of Social Policy and Intervention, University of Oxford, and a former director of Child Poverty Action Group.

Mike Brewer is Chief Economist at the Resolution Foundation and a Professor of Economics at the University of Essex.

Alan Buckle is Chair of Child Poverty Action Group and a director of Tax Justice UK. He was previously Deputy Chair of KPMG.

Kristie Carter is Director of the Child Poverty Unit, Department of the Prime Minister and Cabinet, New Zealand.

John Dickie is Director of Child Poverty Action Group in Scotland.

Paul Dornan is an independent researcher, who has been working with All Together in Dignity / ATD Fourth World UK.

Naomi Eisenstadt is a visiting research fellow at the University of Oxford and the London School of Economics and was the first Director of the Sure Start Unit.

Lizzie Flew is Senior Communications and Campaigns Officer at Child Poverty Action Group.

Alison Garnham is Chief Executive of Child Poverty Action Group.

Sophie Howes is Senior Policy and Research Officer at Child Poverty Action Group.

Omar Khan is Director of the Runnymede Trust.

Karen Laing is Senior Research Associate and Co-Director of the Centre for Learning and Teaching at Newcastle University.

Tom Lee is Senior Policy Analyst at Child Poverty Action Group.

Ruth Lister is Emeritus Professor of Social Policy, Loughborough University and a member of the House of Lords. She is a former director of Child Poverty Action Group and is now its honorary president.

Gill Main is an Associate Professor at the School of Education, University of Leeds.

Jane Millar is Professor of Social Policy at the University of Bath.

Polly Neate is CEO of Shelter, the housing and homelessness charity.

Carey Oppenheim is project-lead on Early Childhood at the Nuffield Foundation, former Chief Executive of the Early Intervention Foundation and was special advisor to former Prime Minister Tony Blair.

Cara Pacitti is a Researcher at the Resolution Foundation.

Jonathan Portes is Professor of Economics and Public Policy, King's College London.

Tess Ridge is Professor Emeritus of Social Policy at the University of Bath.

Diana Skelton is part of the National Coordination Team of All Together in Dignity / ATD Fourth World UK and an expert contributor to the Global Coalition to End Child Poverty.

Kitty Stewart is Associate Professor of Social Policy at the London School of Economics and Political Science and Associate Director of the Centre for Analysis of Social Exclusion.

David Taylor-Robinson is Professor of Public Health and Policy at the University of Liverpool and Honorary Consultant in Child Public Health at Alder Hey Children's Hospital.

Liz Todd is Professor of Educational Inclusion and Director of Institute for Social Science at Newcastle University.

Contents

Foreword

Gordon Brown

The work done over two-thirds of a century by the Child Poverty Action Group has been, and is, inspirational and I am privileged to have been involved with CPAG over the last four decades. It was, and remains, the UK's main charity exposing the scourge of child poverty, mobilising support for children in the country, with its energies targeted on changing policy in government. Set up in 1965 to campaign against the evils of poverty, it was never under any illusions: its purpose could never be achieved until all forms of child poverty were ended.

So, it is a tragedy that the 2020s will become the decade where there are more children in poverty than during the Thatcher-Major years, more than at any time since CPAG was created – and a stain on the soul of our country.

Twenty years ago, in 1999, not least because of the campaigning by CPAG, our Labour government officially dedicated itself to the war against child poverty. We promised that a year later, in spring 2000, we would publish an ambitious timetable to meet the goal of ending child poverty in twenty years and that in subsequent Budgets we would expand the radical new measures essential to its abolition.

Our plan started with a determination to break the two-decade-long rise in child poverty – and then, stage by stage, eliminate child poverty. We were so deeply committed to abolition that we bound ourselves in a law that required us to halve child poverty by 2010 on the road to eventually ending it in 2020.

Indeed, there was a point at which the ending of child poverty was within our country's grasp. By 2010, according to recent Resolution Foundation figures, 1.4 million children had been lifted out of poverty by a combination of child benefit rises and child tax credits along with low unemployment and the minimum wage, and recent in-depth academic research has confirmed that we came very close to reaching our interim target of halving child poverty by 2010.

But to halve child poverty was never, for us, a cause for complacency. At the start of 2010, I expressed my determination to do more to end child poverty by this year.

Unfortunately, in the most recent of times, child poverty has suffered an almost inexorable rise. By 2019, child poverty had risen from three million in 2015 to four million and recent projections vary from the Resolution Foundation projection of 4.8 million by 2023–2024 to the Institute for Fiscal Studies (IFS) estimate of 5.2 million by 2023–2024, both shameful statistics that suggest child poverty is now of epidemic proportions.

But this rise in child poverty has been no accident, nor just the outcome from years of slow economic growth: it has been the direct result of the freeze in child benefit and tax credits, the two-child limit on child tax credit claims, scrapping the family element of child tax credits, decreasing a ceiling on housing benefit help and the disaster that is universal credit.

It is the human costs people have to pay as a result of worsening poverty that angers me most: families forced to depend on food banks, bedding banks, clothes banks, hygiene banks and baby banks; families too poor to afford what we consider the most basic necessities in life; families split up because of the effects of poverty – and children going to school ill-clad and hungry, without hope of better opportunities in the years to come.

There is, in the words of one writer, despair in the communities government ministers never visit, and desolation etched on the faces of people they never see. None of us can feel comfortable when nearly five million children lack basic comforts; not one of us can be at ease when millions of families are increasingly ill at ease; and no one can ever feel secure when so many more families are about to become much more insecure.

Why are we now going in the wrong direction on child poverty? The truth is that the benefits cuts are one element in the breakdown of the 75-year-old post-war social contract.

Its four pillars are now in a state of collapse.

First, for millions, work no longer pays. Twenty-five years ago, child poverty was rising because of unemployment. Today it is rising fastest because of low pay. In fact, two-thirds of children in poverty – that's nearly three million children – are in poverty because their family's breadwinner is paid far too little to make ends meet.

Second, no matter how hard you strive, opportunities for upward mobility seem limited and for people from families on low incomes there appears to be less room at the top. Parents no longer feel confident that the next generation will do as well as the last.

Third, extremes of wealth used to be justified on the basis of merit, effort and contributions to the community. Now such inequalities in income and wealth cannot be explained away – as once they were – by claiming that the huge remuneration packages that business and city elites receive are the result of their hard work. Excessive boardroom remuneration packages, the bankers' bonus culture and shocking extremes of inequality have put paid to any such defence.

Fourthly, our 75-year-old safety net looks threadbare, as, in every town and city, child poverty and homelessness are on the increase as universal credit – which started off as an attempt to paper over the cracks – has exposed how profound the injustices and insecurities that people face today are. Instead of our welfare state offering an adequate safety net, charity is fast becoming the last line of defence for Britain's child poor.

And the new national poverty figures to be released just after this book is published will repeat this sad story – one ministers will not want to hear but one they surely cannot ignore.

If future poverty figures are in line with the latest estimates of the brilliant organisations campaigning for children's rights, the Child Poverty Action Group itself, their academic advisers, the IFS, the Resolution Foundation and the Joseph Rowntree Foundation, then we will find that during the 2020s poverty among children will continue to rise. Indeed, one survey suggests that nine out of every 10 children in non-working households will soon be in poverty – a staggering 40 per cent higher than in 2010. Very soon two in every three children in single-parent households and almost as many in households with three children or more will face poverty.

What should we do? First, we need an urgent review of universal credit on the lines suggested by the Child Poverty Action Group and we must hear the voices of those who know what it is like to have help removed or reduced. And to halt the rising epidemic, child benefit – the basic building block for all we do – should be raised and child tax credits should be restored. The unjust two-child benefit limit that penalises innocent children should be scrapped. To tackle low family incomes that arise from low pay in the workplace, we also need substantial rises in the minimum and living wage.

In 2015, Child Poverty Action Group celebrated its 50th anniversary and it was an honour to be invited to give a lecture to celebrate this occasion. At this time, I argued that CPAG has even more work to do than when founded in 1965 and that even if the current government will not yet give the country its plan for addressing poverty, it was right for CPAG to publish and push its own: to address the new challenges of insecure work resulting in low incomes, of changing technology, and of inadequate family support and the new pressures on children's lives, including poor health, poor educational outcomes and rising mental illness.

It is about justice for all – and about hope. It has been said that you can survive for 40 days without food, eight days without water, eight minutes without air, but only a second without hope. CPAG's campaigning gives us hope. And as CPAG's work testifies, the hope that matters is not simply hope on a wing and a prayer. It cannot just be wishful thinking – that perhaps someday we might be able to do something about child poverty. It cannot be sunny but empty optimism that we can do something about it, but we do not yet know what to do. Hope has to be based on the realistic expectation that we can and will actually change things. And so, hope requires us to mobilise around a programme for change that engages the widest group of mothers, fathers, children and all citizens. CPAG brings life to these ideals, reminding us of our shared goal: not just to take children out of poverty with none left behind, but to be the first generation in history that guarantees to every child the best start in life.

Introduction

Josephine Tucker

Twenty-one years ago, Tony Blair pledged to end child poverty within a generation. Yet after an initial 10 years of progress, today 4.1 million children are once again living in poverty – almost as many as when the pledge was made – and we are set to see record poverty levels in the coming years. The Child Poverty Act, which mandated governments to reduce child poverty and was passed in 2010 with cross-party support, has been wrecked, and since 2012 cuts have been made to financial support for families, the scale of which would once have seemed unimaginable. And with pensioners protected, cuts have fallen most heavily on children and families, despite the fact that children are twice as likely to be poor. There have been over 50 different cuts and restrictions to working-age benefits, chipping away at the support available to struggling families and their children, which will soon add up to a £40 billion annual reduction in the social security budget: the burden of austerity has fallen most heavily on the shoulders of those who can bear it least, as Alison Garnham exposes in our first chapter. Perhaps the most alarming changes are those which have broken the link between assessment of need and entitlement to support, with third children no longer eligible for tax credits or universal credit, and housing support falling far behind rents, among others.

We now have more food banks in the UK than we have branches of McDonald's, teachers are warning of children arriving at school hungry, and rough sleepers are returning to streets up and down the country. And work is too often not enough to protect families from poverty – 70 per cent of children in poverty have working parents. We therefore cannot avoid spending some time in this book examining the damage done, and what it means for children in the UK today, before turning our attention to the future and where we need to go next. Tom Lee starts by analysing the impact of cuts on family incomes and shows that not only is the *number* of children in poverty rising, but families in poverty are falling further and further below the poverty line every year, particularly lone parents (Chapter 2). Torsten Bell and Cara Pacitti discuss how – despite high employment and increases in the minimum wage – even *absolute* poverty has started to creep up as wages stagnate and social security cuts bring down living standards (Chapter 4). This is unprecedented in recent decades.

We know that when tax credits were increased in the early 2000s, the extra money families had was spent on things which are good for children,[1] and that changes in family income have a powerful causal effect on children's wellbeing, health and education.[2] In Chapter 3, Jonathan Bradshaw draws on international data to show that when the UK invested in reducing child poverty in the 2000s, children's wellbeing went up on a host of measures, taking the UK from near the bottom to the middle of international league tables. We do not yet have comparative data to put the impacts of today's levels of child poverty into international comparison, but it is clear that on many indicators, child wellbeing in the UK is now getting worse. David Taylor-Robinson (Chapter 15) explains that while health inequalities narrowed significantly when the government acted to tackle them, health disparities between richer and poorer parts of the country are now rising again. Progress on life expectancy has stalled, mental health is worsening, and infant mortality is rising, particularly in deprived areas.

Not all families and children face the same poverty risks, and the poverty statistics reveal huge differences in the rates of poverty among children of different ethnic backgrounds. It is shocking that more than half the UK's Bangladeshi and Pakistani children, and nearly half of black children, live below the poverty line compared with just over a quarter of white children. Omar Khan (Chapter 10) discusses the reasons for this, and argues that both government and campaigners need to be brave enough to acknowledge the issue of race when talking about child poverty, and to develop analyses of poverty which properly consider it.

It is not just financial support for families which has faced the axe. Sure Start centres, extended schools, public health services and local authority funding have all been hollowed out, which combine with loss of income to deadly effect. And no government since the 1999 pledge has done enough to increase the supply of genuinely affordable housing, leaving families at the mercy of soaring rents and poor housing security and now – as help with housing costs has been cut – pushing rising numbers of children into homelessness, as described by Polly Neate in Chapter 16.

But despite all this, we do not want this book to be all doom and gloom. We must not forget about the good things that have been achieved over the past 20 years – there is much we can learn and much we can hold on to, celebrate and build on. One thing is certain: we have proven that with active policy support and investment, the government could bring an end to child poverty. And progress has not fallen back on all fronts. Recent years have seen the introduction of shared parental leave and the expansion of free childcare provision for 2–4-year-olds, discussed by Naomi

Eisenstadt and Carey Oppenheim in Chapter 12. These are good steps, despite serious concerns about who is able to benefit and whether the *quantity* of early years education is expanding at the expense of *quality*. There is also more financial support for working families than there was 20 years ago, despite heavy cuts in recent years and despite all the well-documented problems which universal credit creates for working parents.

While child poverty targets have been scrapped, campaigners did salvage a commitment to publish poverty statistics every year, which is now enshrined in law. And the understanding that poverty is relative, and is fundamentally about money, also seems to have been saved, despite a politically engineered controversy over both these questions in the middle of this decade, as Jonathan Portes discusses in Chapter 7.

So, what will it take to end child poverty today? We need an urgent programme of investment in children, particularly financial support for families. Mike Brewer describes what this might entail in Chapter 6, calling for an immediate end to the two-child limit, an end to policies targeting particular groups like the benefit cap and lower universal credit rates for parents under 25, and a renewed commitment to ensure support rises with inflation. We also need a renewed national commitment to ending child poverty, in whatever form this takes. Lizzie Flew discusses the history of child poverty strategies over the last 20 years and maps out key elements of a possible new UK strategy (Chapter 20), arguing that cross-sectoral action is needed – which is why all contributors to this book have been asked to reflect on what needs to happen next – and that targets matter.

John Dickie asks what can be learned from Scotland, which has diverged from the UK government this decade and adopted much of what we want to see countrywide (extra support for children, targets enshrined in law, and a human rights-based approach), although policies announced so far by the Scottish government will be limited in their impact (Chapter 19). We must also draw inspiration from around the world and we are delighted that Prime Minister Jacinda Ardern of New Zealand and the Director of New Zealand's Child Poverty Unit, Kristie Carter, have contributed a chapter explaining how they are tackling child poverty as part of a comprehensive child wellbeing strategy (Chapter 21), developed out of a real commitment to ensure all children in New Zealand are involved and with an ambition that theirs should be among the best childhoods in the world.

In the slightly longer term, we need to have a thorough public discussion about what sort of social security system we want, and how the system can be redesigned to provide real security for families and children. In Chapter 18, Sophie Howes discusses the principles that should underpin a reimagined social security system – prevention and reduction of poverty, income security, and social solidarity – and asks whether we need to put brakes on the ever-increasing focus on means testing if we are to achieve these, and if so how. Universal credit seems, in many ways, to be taking us in the wrong direction.

Jane Millar and Tess Ridge give us much to draw on in this debate from the perspective of lone parents and their experiences over the last 16 years (Chapter 5). Lone parents have borne the brunt of cuts and faced an increasingly punitive system of work-related conditionality. Research indicates they would be much better served with personalised, supportive coaching for those ready to work (as most have a high commitment to working already), unconditional help to stabilise families who have escaped domestic violence or recently separated, and a benefits system which provides adequate and reliable payments. It is also clear that young people need much more support when becoming independent.

Fran Bennett and Ruth Lister consider the particular question of what a revived universalist agenda might look like in Chapter 13, and how this could provide a platform of financial support and services for all children, on which families can build their future. We need to move away from stigmatising initiatives targeting the poorest – whether through the benefits system or programmes like so-called 'holiday hunger' clubs – and pursue models that bring children and families together and help to build a more equal society – one in which we are truly all in it together.

On a similar note, Karen Laing and Liz Todd (Chapter 14) argue that we must do more to ensure that education is truly inclusive. This means focusing on assets – the positive contributions which children and communities bring – rather than deficits, prioritising inclusion and wellbeing over test scores, making sure that the costs associated with schooling do not put pressure on families and removing inadvertent stigma affecting students on a low income, for example around receipt of free school meals. There is also evidence that extended schools and approaches such as children's communities, in which schools work with others in the community to provide wraparound and holiday activities and childcare, and to support children 'from cradle to career', can be transformative.

The coming years will bring many challenges. Unless there is a significant change of course, benefit cuts will continue to bring down living standards and child poverty will continue to rise. On top of this, Brexit is likely to have economic consequences which will be felt nationwide but will particularly affect the areas where child poverty is already rising fastest, as well as putting employment rights at risk and putting ever greater pressure on services such as healthcare which rely on European workers, as Kitty Stewart sets out in Chapter 11. It is vital that children are protected from economic risks and that families already hit hard by cuts are not dealt a further blow.

Our new government came into power with a promise to address child poverty, and to 'level up' the nation. If this is a serious ambition, the experience of the last 20 years shows what can be done and gives us many lessons about how to do it. Funding this effort would not be difficult with political will; as Alan Buckle explores in Chapter 17 there are many options at the Chancellor's disposal for raising revenue. Indeed, alongside the cuts to social security this decade, a similar amount has been spent on raising personal tax allowances which primarily benefit the better off.

Finally, any strategy must take account of the views of people with lived experience of life on a low income. We have therefore devoted two chapters to discussion of ways to bring forward the voice of experts by experience. Paul Dornan and Diana Skelton, writing on behalf of ATD Fourth World, present principles which have been developed through a participatory process, which any child poverty strategy needs to take on board (Chapter 9). These recognise that while money is central to poverty, poverty also means experiencing a lack of control, stigma, negative judgements and interactions with disempowering systems and policies. If people in poverty play a key role in talking about and responding to it, the effect can be transformative.

As Gill Main observes in Chapter 8, bringing together findings from several projects involving work with children, young people and parents on a low income, people are asking for entirely reasonable things, but too often do not feel heard by those with the power to take decisions affecting their lives:

> 'People want safe places to live, free from the fear of crime and with police forces they can trust. They want good educational opportunities for children, and good employment opportunities for parents. They want affordable and accessible services like doctors, job centres, and careers advisers. They want to be paid fairly for work, and to be able to rely on an adequate safety net when things go wrong. They want houses which are well maintained and which do not pose a threat to their health. They want accountability in how the media and politicians talk about them. This list of demands is hardly excessive or complicated.'

We have the tools to ensure that all children in the UK have a decent standard of living and can achieve wellbeing. Ending child poverty is the place to start. CPAG will continue campaigning until no child has to live in poverty and no family is excluded from society through a lack of these fundamentals. It is time for policy makers to listen and step up.

Notes and references

1   P Gregg, J Waldfogel and E Washbrook, 'That's the way it goes: expenditure patterns as real incomes rise for the poorest families with children', in J Hills and K Stewart, *A More Equal Society? New Labour, poverty, inequality and exclusion*, Policy Press, 2005

2   K Cooper and K Stewart, 'Does money affect children's outcomes? An update', CASE paper 203, London School of Economics, 2017; and K Cooper and K Stewart, *Does Money Affect Children's Outcomes? A systematic review*, Joseph Rowntree Foundation, 2013

One

Progress made and policy in retreat?

Alison Garnham

When your government names its chief ambition as ending child poverty – that counts as a crowning achievement for an organisation called the Child Poverty Action Group – the clue is in the name. The strategy, announced on 18 March 1999 at Toynbee Hall by Tony Blair, set government departments racing to put it into action – led by the Treasury. Yet, the Child Poverty Act, which wrote the strategy into binding law, and enacted in 2010, was eventually abolished in 2016. The only thing rescued from the parliamentary flames was the continuing duty to publish the annual child poverty indicators. So what did the strategy achieve, what remains of those efforts and what have we learned from it?

The truth is a lot of progress was made. Child poverty fell by over one million,[1] levels of debt and deprivation fell and child wellbeing improved.[2] In fact, child wellbeing improved on 36 out of 48 OECD indicators. We saw the biggest falls in child poverty in the whole of the OECD between the mid-1990s and 2008. Families spent more on fruit and vegetables, children's clothes and books and less on tobacco and alcohol;[3] and parental employment rates rose, particularly for lone parents with rates rising from 45 to 57 per cent and continuing to grow afterwards to the present rate of 70 per cent.[4] The educational attainment gap began to close.[5]

None of this was just a lucky by-product of a buoyant employment market. Money was invested in child benefit and tax credits, making work pay and families better off. A national minimum wage was introduced. The 'new deals' provided employment support for young people, people with disabilities and lone parents. The new deal for lone parents (NDLP) was a voluntary scheme that doubled lone parents' chances of getting into paid work. There was a national childcare strategy and the first ever Childcare Act in 2006. These heralded a new, free entitlement for three- and four-year-olds, investment to increase the number of childcare places and a plan for comprehensive extended schools' provision from 8am to 6pm and throughout the school holidays. Childcare quality would be raised through improved qualifications, the enhanced professional status of providers and through the early years foundation stage (EYFS). Together with new funding, these raised the quantity and quality of early childhood education and care.

Sure Start, culminating in children's centres, was another critical infrastructure investment. Crucially, across all government departments, child poverty was a top priority, including in health, social care and schools, and with professionals encouraged to work together towards shared objectives, including ending child poverty, under the shared banner of 'Every Child Matters'.

We learned a lot. It turned out that child poverty is indeed policy responsive. If you do the right things the numbers fall, and when you stop doing them, they rise. Change is achievable and it is entirely realistic to set targets to end child poverty. Setting targets works. Tony Blair said: 'And I will set out our historic aim that ours is the first generation to end child poverty for ever, and it will take a generation. It is a 20-year mission but I believe it can be done.' And he was right. Had we stayed the course, we would have hit the target (see Chapter 2).

So why are we now so far from achieving the 20-year target? A lot was achieved, but results for the 10-year target did not come in until 2012 due to the time lag in publishing poverty figures. It turned out, by 2010, we were halfway to achieving the target to end child poverty.[6] And new Labour had not been good at communicating its efforts and much had been achieved by stealth – known as 'talking *Daily Mail* and acting *Guardian*'. Apart from delighted service users with young children, much of the public were entirely unaware of the project. Then came deficit reduction under the coalition in 2010. In the Budget and Spending Review of 2010, some £80 billion of cuts to benefits and services were announced, with over £20 billion in benefit cuts – and a further £15 billion of benefit cuts to come in the July 2015 Budget (which included destroying the poverty-fighting potential of the nascent universal credit).

According to the Office for Budget Responsibility (OBR) analysis, we are already spending £36 billion less on social security than in 2010, and by 2023/24 the loss will reach £40 billion.[7] Justified as deficit reduction, it was never explained why 85 per cent of savings were to come from cuts to benefits and services compared to a mere 15 per cent in tax rises. It was claimed at the time that 'those with the broadest shoulders' would bear the biggest burden and that 'we are all in it together'. Evidently, some have been 'in it' far more than anybody else.

There have of course been significant increases since 2010 in the national minimum wage (NMW) reducing the number of people on low pay, plus significant amounts have been spent on raising the personal tax allowance. Although presented as a pro-poor policy, this latter, expensive policy is not well targeted, with around 80 per cent going to the richest half of the income distribution.[8] For many low-income families, net income is determined by the level of means-tested benefits such as tax credits and universal credit. Not all increases in the national minimum wage lead to big income improvements, with most clawed back through the relevant benefit withdrawal rate – otherwise known as the poverty trap. Middle-income families, particularly those with a second earner, feel the benefit more.

Across the EU, a few countries stand out as having higher child poverty rates before the tax and benefit system kicks in – including the UK and Ireland.[9] After tax and benefits, the UK child poverty rate falls to around the middle range in the EU – with our tax and benefit system doing most of the heavy lifting in bringing down high child poverty rates to middling ones. Therefore, incomes in the UK are particularly sensitive to changes in taxes and benefits, as are poverty rates. Given the Child Poverty Act had been passed with all-party agreement in March 2010, and the extent of modelling work that had taken place in the Treasury, there could have been little doubt what the impact of cuts this size would mean for child poverty numbers.

Detractors have mocked the idea of writing into law the ambition to end child poverty – pointless if already government policy, or a disingenuous attempt to hog-tie future governments? Whatever your view, it did keep the issue on the agenda long after the new government had lost interest. And, despite announced benefit cuts, child poverty was slow to rise initially because the child tax credit had been boosted after the 2008 crash, quite deliberately to protect the poorest from the expected economic fallout. Whether the Act was useful or not, having an official government target has certainly inspired others across the world[10] – seeing the setting up of the Child Poverty Action Group USA, and new targets and a child wellbeing strategy in New Zealand (see also Chapter 21), in Canada and heightened interest from the European Commission.

Also, despite recent government efforts to redefine poverty as being about personal or family characteristics, the overwhelming response to the last government consultation on measurement showed almost universal agreement that poverty was indeed about a lack of resources and was a relative concept.[11] This unanimity continues in the latest cross-party effort – the Social Metrics Commission. For the future, any new strategy would also need to avoid the popular trap of dividing a lack of resources or deprivations into 'the poverties' (food, clothing, period, fuel, water, digital, transport, financial access, furniture, appliance poverty) with in-kind, charitable solutions deemed an appropriate response. They are all just poverty – manifestations of the deprivation caused by a lack of income. We do not have a lack of food in the UK, we are actually facing a child poverty crisis.

This may be the last opportunity to remind people what can be achieved with a shared purpose and concentrated effort and resources – and that we demonstrated this in the UK. A lesson for today would be to communicate intentions and engage the public and families in poverty to ensure popular buy-in. A strategy for today would look a little different (see Chapter 20), but we need to make the case for it once again and with more urgency than ever before.

Notes and references

1   Department for Work and Pensions, *Households Below Average Income: an analysis of UK income distribution, 1994/95–2017/18*, 2019

2   J Bradshaw, 'Child wellbeing in the 2000s', in L Judge (ed), *Ending Child Poverty by 2020: progress made and lessons learned*, CPAG, 2012

3   P Gregg, J Waldfogel and E Washbrook, 'That's the way it goes: expenditure patterns as real incomes rise for the poorest families with children', in J Hills and K Stewart, *A More Equal Society? New Labour, poverty, inequality and exclusion*, Policy Press, 2005

4   K Stewart, 'Child poverty: what have we really achieved?', in L Judge (ed), *Ending Child Poverty by 2020: progress made and lessons learned*, CPAG, 2012; and Office for National Statistics, *Working and Workless Households: April–June 2019*, Table P, 2019

5   D Hirsch, 'Better off, better educated', in L Judge (ed), *Ending Child Poverty by 2020: progress made and lessons learned*, CPAG, 2012

6   We were halfway to 10 per cent, which according to the targets was the point at which child poverty would be deemed to have been eradicated, although strangely the government actually set itself the target to be halfway to zero. And, according to the Resolution Foundation, we did reach the target but it was hidden because of underreporting of benefit receipt in the Family Resources Survey: A Corlett and others, *The Living Standards Audit 2018*, London: Resolution Foundation, 2018.

7   Author's calculations using Office for Budget Responsibility, Policy Measures Database, March 2019

8   Author's calculations using UKMOD version A1.0+

9   J Bradshaw with T Lee, *Child Poverty and Child Benefits in Europe*, CPAG, 2020, cpag.org.uk/projects/secure-futures; and H Xavier Jara and C Leventi, *Note on EU27 Child Poverty Rates*, research note prepared for CPAG by the Institute for Social and Economic Research (ISER), 2014

10 See, for example: J Waldfogel, *Britain's War on Poverty*, Russell Sage Foundation, 2010

11 K Stewart and N Roberts, *How Do Experts Think Child Poverty should be Measured in the UK? An analysis of the Coalition Government's consultation on child poverty measurement 2012–13*, CASEpaper 197, London School of Economics, 2016

Two

The austerity generation: the extent of the damage

Tom Lee

What's the damage so far?

The 2010 Child Poverty Act imposed a legal duty on governments to produce a child poverty strategy and to move towards four UK-wide targets by
2020. However, the government's actions since 2010 have in fact led to an
increase in child poverty. The Coalition and Conservative governments
pursued a fiscal programme of austerity that has consisted of sustained
reductions in public spending across a variety of areas. Most notably for child
poverty, a succession of government policies reduced the level of financial
support provided through the social security system. The Office for Budget
Responsibility (OBR) estimates the total effect of government policies
announced since 2010 is a forecasted £36 billion reduction in social security
spending by 2019/20, and a £40 billion reduction by 2023/24.[1] This chapter
asks what has happened to child poverty across the decade, how much of
it can be attributed to government policy and what could be done differently?

Figure 2.1 shows how child poverty, measured as the number of
children whose equivalised household income is below 60 per cent of the
median household, evolved from 2010/11 to 2017/18 (the latest year for
which we have poverty numbers).[2] The government's relative income
poverty target was to reduce the share of children in relative poverty
before housing costs (BHC) poverty to 10 per cent (1.4 million) by 2020.

From 2010/11 to 2013/14 the number of children in poverty stayed
fairly constant, for both the BHC and after housing costs (AHC) measures.
This was driven by both real household median income and incomes for
families at the bottom of the income distribution falling at the same rate
following the financial crisis. Falling incomes at the bottom of the income
distribution push more people into poverty, while a fall in median household income means the poverty threshold is mechanically lowered, bringing some people out of poverty. The net effect was no change in the
number of children in poverty.

Figure 2.1:

Number of children in poverty before and after housing costs

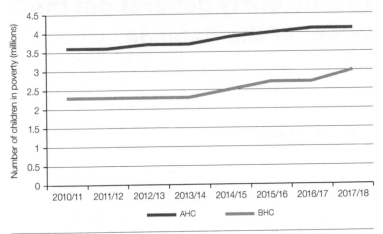

Source: Department for Work and Pensions, *Households Below Average Income* (HBAI) statistics

Since 2013/14, median household income has grown faster than household incomes further down the income distribution. This had led to a rise in the number of children in poverty. Although slow growth in incomes at the bottom of the income distribution can be partially attributed to factors such as a precarious labour market, a key contributor is austerity. A variety of measures including below inflation increases in benefits, cutting the level of financial support in tax credits and reducing entitlements in universal credit led to incomes stagnating at the bottom of the income distribution. In 2017/18 there were three million children in BHC poverty, 600,000 more than in 2010/11. Similarly, once housing costs are taken into account, there were over four million children in poverty in 2017/18, 500,000 more than in 2010/11 and reaching 30 per cent of all the country's children.

However, it is not just the number of children in poverty that is important. It is also vital to know how far families are below the poverty line. Figure 2.2 shows how the median poverty gap (how far the average family in poverty is below the poverty line) has changed since 2010/11. The increase in the depth of poverty is even starker than the rise in the number of children in poverty. From 2012/13 to 2017/18, the real AHC median poverty gap rose by 30 per cent. The story of the decade is more children in poverty, while those in poverty are further away from escaping it.

Figure 2.2:

Median poverty gap for families before and after housing costs

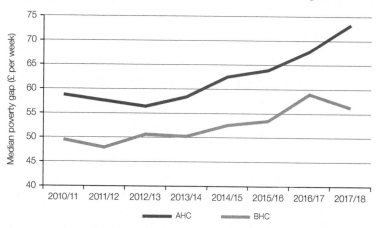

Note: The figure shows the equivalised (adjusted for household size) real (controlling for inflation) median poverty gap – 2017/18 prices.

Source: Author's calculations using Department for Work and Pensions, *Households Below Average Income* (HBAI) statistics

Have we seen all the damage yet?

The rate and depth of poverty is only likely to increase in the future. A key reason behind this increase is that many austerity measures had not taken full effect by 2017/18. For instance, the OBR estimates that the majority of the reduction in social security spending due to the benefit freeze was in the past two years, making it highly likely that we will see an increase in child poverty in 2018/19 (the statistics have not been released at the time of writing) and 2019/20.

For other policies, the full effect will be felt even further in the future. The two-child limit has not yet had a large impact on poverty as it only applies to children born after April 2017. Over time, the number of children affected by this policy will increase substantially. In addition, the next few years will see many families who currently claim legacy benefits move over to universal credit. It is therefore worth looking at the effect of austerity on child poverty in 2023/24.

Estimates indicate that, even if there are no additional cuts to social security, by 2023/24 the number of children in AHC poverty could reach 4.8 million, the highest number since records began.[3]

Some policies have a particular effect on child poverty. The two-child limit will mean that an additional 300,000 children are in poverty by 2023/24 as well as pushing a million children deeper into poverty, while the benefit freeze means that 200,000 extra children will be in poverty in 2023/24.[4] The benefit cap only has a small effect on the number of children in poverty, as most of these children would be below the poverty line anyway. However, it does mean that by 2023/24 an estimated 400,000 children will be deeper in poverty. The total effect of the two-child limit, benefit freeze (including loss in value of child benefit since 2009/10), benefit cap and loss of first child premium is 700,000 more children in poverty by 2023/24, as well as millions of children deeper in poverty. On average, households with children lose a £1,000 a year as a result of these austerity policies. The estimated cost of scrapping these policies is £8.3 billion, a small fraction of the total cuts to social security spending since 2010.

Evidence from the last decade shows that reducing support for families through the social security system leads to a rise in child poverty. But the years immediately following Tony Blair's 1999 pledge to end child poverty tell us that we can reverse this trend. Figure 2.3 shows how the number of children in BHC poverty has evolved, compared to what would have been required to eliminate child poverty by 2020 in line with Tony Blair's 1999 pledge.[5]

Can the damage be reversed?

From 1999/2000 to 2004/05, the fall in child poverty was broadly in line with the trajectory required. This large reduction was primarily due to sustained real increases in entitlements to social security, particularly for families with children. For instance, from 1999/2000 to 2004/05 a lone parent with one child in part-time work saw her/his cash value of benefits increase by nearly 50 per cent, substantially more than the increase in median household income.[6] From 2005/06 to 2007/08 (ie, even pre-recession/austerity), social security entitlements rose only at the rate of inflation, which led to child poverty no longer falling.[7]

This shows that poverty is policy responsive. Increases in the generosity of social security led to the child poverty rate falling, while austerity had the opposite effect. It can be argued that increasing the generosity of the social security is easier when times are good. To some extent this is true as more people are in work and tax revenues are higher. However, when the economy is booming, median household income is probably also rising.

Figure 2.3:

Number of children in relative BHC poverty compared to elimination trajectory

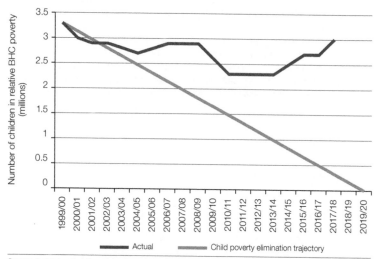

Source: Author's calculations using Department for Work and Pensions, *Households Below Average Income* (HBAI) statistics

This means that there is even more need to make household incomes at the bottom of the income distribution grow faster than median income.

Austerity has led to an increase in child poverty over the last decade, although the effects have been mitigated somewhat by slow growth in median household income, with more to come as austerity policy measures take full effect. If the social security system remains in its current state, hundreds of thousands more children will be pushed into poverty over the next few years. However, it is not yet too late to reverse this rise in poverty. Increasing entitlements to social security at the bottom of the income distribution can lift millions of children out of poverty.

Notes and references

1 Author's calculations from the Policy Measures Database, Office for Budget Responsibility, March 2019

2 Although some people favour other measures, the focus of this chapter will be relative household income measures. An income-based measure means value judgements do not have to be made about what is an 'acceptable standard of living'. A relative measure means that poverty is relative to how well the economy is doing. As the economy grows, there is

more money to go round and expectations over what constitutes poverty change.

3   L Gardiner, *The Shifting Shape of Social Security: charting the size and shape of the British welfare system*, Resolution Foundation, 2019

4   All estimates of specific measures come from J Tucker, *Universal Credit: what needs to change to reduce child poverty and make it fit for families?*, CPAG, 2019

5   A relative before housing costs (BHC) poverty measure is used as this was the favoured measure in 1999.

6   M Brewer and others, *Child Poverty in the UK since 1998–99: lessons from the past decade*, Working Paper 10/23, Institute for Fiscal Studies, 2010

7   Child poverty fell substantially from 2008/09 to 2010/11 due to a large reduction in median household income. Automatic stabilisers mean that, in a recession, median household income is likely to fall by more than incomes at the bottom of the income distribution.

Three

Child poverty and child wellbeing: comparative evidence

Jonathan Bradshaw

In more optimistic moments than now, those engaged in policy research may hope that the comparative evidence about child poverty which emerged in the late 1970s[1] as well as the comparative studies of family benefits[2] that were published about the same time might have influenced the Toynbee Hall announcement in 1999 that child poverty in the UK would be eradicated. The evidence showed that the UK child poverty rate was well above the national average of rich countries and that family benefits and social assistance payments were comparatively far from generous.

One might also hope that the comparative research that began to emerge on child outcomes and child wellbeing[3] might have influenced the Department for Work and Pensions in publishing *Opportunities for All* and the introduction of the 'Every Child Matters' agenda. Surely the comparative work that culminated in the first UNICEF Innocenti Report Card 7[4] comparing child wellbeing in OECD countries, using data from the late 1990s which found the UK at the bottom of the international league table, caused a stir.

The case for comparison remains a strong one, however difficult the enterprise. National statistics can tell us whether we are getting better or worse, but without comparison we cannot know how well or badly we are doing or how good or bad we could become. These issues inspired this chapter.

The comparative evidence on child poverty and child wellbeing has become much better than it was 25 years ago. The EU Statistics on Income and Living Conditions (EU-SILC) (and Office for National Statistics promises to sustain the UK data after Brexit) are published annually, data from the Health Behaviour in School-aged Children (HBSC) survey are published every four years, and the OECD (PISA) survey of education every three years. UNICEF's Office for Research has used these and other sources to publish comparative report cards on child outcomes almost annually since 1997 and the OECD also now publishes a child wellbeing index. As for comparisons of policy, the OECD tax benefit model has improved a lot, and EUROMOD has launched a tax and benefit policy module.

What does the most up-to-date comparative evidence on child poverty tell us (according to EU-SILC)?

- In 2018, the UK had the third highest pre-transfer child poverty rate (that is, before the impact of taxes and benefits) out of 29 European countries. See Figure 3.1 below.

Figure 3.1:

Child poverty rates (net income less than 60 per cent median before transfers) (children under 18)

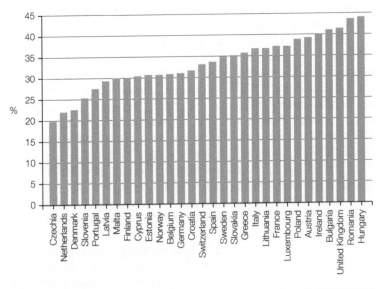

Source: Eurostat database, https://ec.europa.eu/eurostat/data/database

- In 2018, the UK post-transfer child poverty rates was the fifth highest out of 30 European countries, only exceeded by Italy, Bulgaria, Spain and Romania.

- Between 2009 and 2018, the UK was one of more than half of all 29 European countries to have an increase in its child poverty rate. Indeed, the UK had the sixth largest increase. See Figure 3.2.

- The consistent poverty rate (which combines relative low income and a deprivation index) in 2017 was in the middle of the league table of European countries but higher than many poorer countries.

Figure 3.2:

Child poverty rates in 2009 and 2018 with countries ranked by per cent change (children under 18)

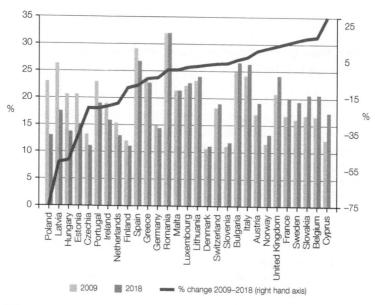

Source: Eurostat database, https://ec.europa.eu/eurostat/data/database

What does the comparative data on child benefits tell us (according to the OECD tax-benefit web calculator)?

- The UK package is comparatively more generous than some other rich countries at lower earnings and for those with no earnings.

- But it needs to be because of the low level of pre-transfer incomes.

- It could be better, and some other quite poor countries have better systems.

- We are now in a minority of countries which effectively do not have a universal child benefit (as high earners have to pay an equivalent tax charge).

What does the comparative evidence on child wellbeing tell us?

- The efforts made by the Labour government shifted the UK from the bottom of the international table on child wellbeing in the 2007 Innocenti Report Card 7 to the middle of the league table in the 2013 Innocenti Report Card 11[5] improving its international ranking from the bottom third to the middle third of countries on poverty, health, behaviour and subjective wellbeing. There was a lot of other evidence that child wellbeing was improving on many fronts.[6]

- There are a variety of indications that child wellbeing has been deteriorating since 2010. Child poverty rates and gaps have increased, infant mortality has stopped falling and social class gaps increased; child homelessness has risen sharply, child mental health and subjective wellbeing have fallen, youth suicide rates are up, and the number of children in care rates is up.

- The next comparative Innocenti Report Card, No.16 is not published until summer 2020, but it is unlikely to show any comparative improvement for the UK and may well have us falling down the league table given the known national trends in child poverty and child outcomes.

In conclusion, the comparative evidence shows that we can do better. We have had lower child poverty rates in the past. We are not doing well on child poverty at present and could do better again.

Notes and references

1   J Bradshaw and J-R Chen, *Poverty in the UK: a comparison with nineteen other countries*, LIS working paper series – No.147, Luxembourg Income Study, 1996

2   T Eardley and others, *Social Assistance in OECD Countries: synthesis report*, Department of Social Security Research Report No.46, 1996; J Bradshaw and others, *Support for Children: A comparison of arrangements in fifteen countries*, Department of Social Security Research Report No.21, 1993

3   J Bradshaw (ed), *Poverty: The outcomes for children*, Family Policy Studies Centre, 2001; G A Cornia, and S Danziger (eds), *Child Poverty and Deprivation in the Industrialized Countries, 1945–1995*, Oxford University Press, 1997

4   UNICEF, *Child Poverty in Perspective: an overview of child well-being in high income countries*, Innocenti Report Card 7, UNICEF Innocenti Research Centre, 2007

5   UNICEF, *Child Well-being in Rich Countries: a comparative overview*, Innocenti Report Card 11, UNICEF Office of Research, 2013

6   J Bradshaw (ed), *The Well-being of Children in the UK*, 4th Edition, Policy Press, 2016

Four

Rising child poverty, wage stagnation and working families

Torsten Bell and Cara Pacitti

Introduction

Child poverty in the UK doubled in the 1980s, from 15 to 30 per cent. Despite ups and downs, it has been stubbornly high ever since. But that stubbornness should not lead us to conclude that it is unchanging. The causes and nature of poverty change far more than either the headlines or common simplistic stories suggest.

As we start a new decade, it is important to reflect on what happened in the last decade in which child poverty was meant to be eradicated. Two trends stand out alongside the shameful fact that relative child poverty rose every year from 2011/12 to 2016/17: first, poverty is now overwhelmingly a question of working poverty and, second, absolute poverty[1] falling fast can no longer be taken for granted. The meaning of these two trends – which are far more intertwined than is generally recognised – their drivers and what they tell us about our future is the subject of this chapter.

The story told of child poverty in Britain has its roots in the 1980s, when fast but regressive income growth caused the top to pull away from the middle but also the middle to pull away from the bottom. The latter trend is what drove the increase in relative child poverty, which increases in social security spending on children during the 2000s put into reverse. The dominant narrative around child poverty has been that predistribution,[2] or the market economy, drives poverty up while redistribution attempts to bring it back down.

Absolute poverty

But that is not the story of the 2010s. The middle has not been pulling away from the bottom. In fact, noone has been doing any pulling away. Wages today are only just returning to their pre-crisis peak a full 12 years on.

That has meant that families with children reached the late 2010s with incomes broadly where they had been in the mid-2000s, as Figure 4.1 shows. Incomes grew by under 5 per cent for children under three (by virtue of being in families) over those 12 years, compared to 40 per cent from the mid-1990s to the mid-2000s.[3]

Figure 4.1:

(Income growth has been sluggish for younger working-age families since the crisis)

Real (CPI-adjusted, 2018/19 terms) median equivalised disposable household income (after housing costs), by age

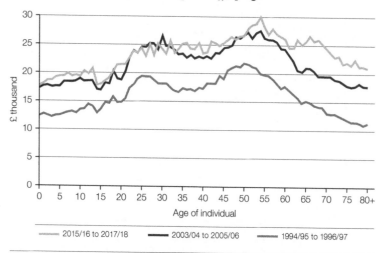

Note: The OECD equivalisation scale assumes children over 13 have higher needs than those under 13. Great Britain before 2002/03, UK from 2002/03 onwards.

Source: Resolution Foundation (RF) analysis of Department for Work and Pensions, *Households Below Average Income* (HBAI) statistics

A growing economy means that absolute poverty should decline over time. But stagnant incomes mean that the progress we have come to take for granted on absolute child poverty (poverty measured against a fixed, rather than relative, real terms poverty line) all but ground to a halt in the 2010s. Figure 4.2 shows that between 2000 and 2007 absolute poverty (using a 2000-based measure) fell eight percentage points (27 per cent); but over the comparable 2010 to 2017 period the 2010-based measure only fell one percentage point (3 per cent). In 2017/18, absolute child poverty actually increased.[4]

Figure 4.2:

(Falls in absolute poverty over previous decades have stagnated since 2010)

Proportion of children living in poverty (after housing costs), for different definitions of poverty

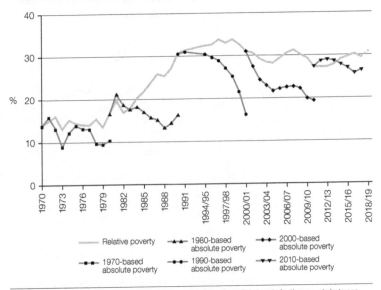

Note: UK data from 2002/03, and before 1994/95, and data for Great Britain only for the years in between. 2018/19 value is a nowcast. 1992 and 1993 values are interpolated due to missing data.

Source: Resolution Foundation analysis of Department for Work and Pensions, *Households Below Average Income* (HBAI) statistics; A Goodman and S Webb, *Institute for Fiscal Studies Households Below Average Income Dataset, 1961–1991*, Resolution Foundation nowcast

In previous decades we have taken falls in absolute poverty for granted, and (rightly) reiterated the damage that rising or high relative child poverty amounts to. It is crucial that we recognise that the lack of income growth in the 2010s translated into no improvement in the living standards of the UK's poorest children. Unequal growth poses very real problems for societies, but no growth is not the answer.

Working poverty

This income stagnation has come despite much more positive minimum wage and employment stories. As a result, low pay is falling significantly for the first time in four decades and over three million more people work today than when the UK was last broadly at full employment in 2008. Moreover, as Figure 4.3 shows, increases in employment have been driven by those with children, especially women.

Figure 4.3:

(More women, particularly mothers, have moved into employment)

16–64-year-old employment rate change, apportioned by sex and family situation: UK, 2007/08 to 2018/19

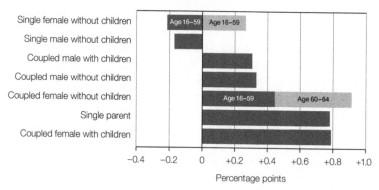

Percentage points

Notes: These figures reflect the employment rate change for each group over the period, weighted according to the average size of the group within the 16–64-year-old population over the period. The prevalence of each of these groups within the working-age adult population barely changed over this period, meaning that this method very closely matches the overall three percentage point increase in the 16–64-year-old employment rate.

Source: Resolution Foundation analysis of Office for National Statistics, quarterly Labour Force Survey

Figure 4.4:

(Child poverty is heading back to highs not seen since the mid-1990s, and may even surpass them)

Proportion of children living in relative poverty (after housing costs)

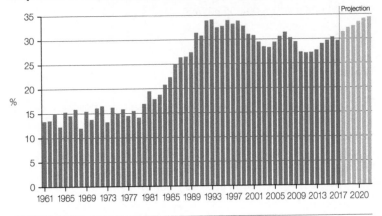

Notes: Financial years after 1993. UK from 2002/03, Great Britain before.

Source: Resolution Foundation analysis of Department for Work and Pensions, *Households Below Average Income* (HBAI) statistics; Resolution Foundation projection; P Bourquin and others, *Living Standards, Poverty and Inequality in the UK: 2019*, Institute for Fiscal Studies, 2019

Growing parental employment should be good news for relative child poverty. That has not happened because, as we shall return to, it has been no match for the opposing pressure from benefit cuts. Instead, the employment trend has completed the transformation of child poverty in twenty-first century Britain into being about working poverty, not the worklessness that followed the recessions of the 1980s and 1990s. Seventy per cent of children living in poverty in 2017/18 had at least one parent in work, up from around half of children in poverty 20 years ago.

This should not be seen as an entirely separate story from the failure to make progress on absolute poverty. Indeed, absolute poverty failing to fall is one of the drivers of the most recent increase in working poverty – many more of us are working,[5] and we are working longer,[6] because we are poorer than we expected to be.

For those with children in, or at risk of poverty, that income stagnation has been about more than the wage squeeze. Our social security system is an estimated £36 billion less generous as a result of policy changes since 2010.[7] These have been focused on poorer working-age families, with the bottom 20 per cent of families losing an average of over 8 per cent of their incomes as a result. This explains why almost all the post-crisis employment gains have been among the poorest third of households, and why the stagnation of absolute poverty and transformation of poverty into working poverty are so closely intertwined.

This also explains why relative poverty has risen in five of the past six years, despite the surge in employment among poorer households.

The 2010s should force us to update our story about child poverty. It is not abstract market forces and growth (predistribution) causing child poverty to rise, it is policy choices on benefits (reverse redistribution). The contrast with both market outcomes and policy choices continuing to drive down pensioner poverty is clear. While almost half of pensioners aged above 75 were living in poverty in the 1960s, relative poverty for this group has since fallen by over two-thirds to below 15 per cent.[8]

Our future

The trends of the 2010s are crucial to understand, because they are not going away. We project that the ongoing roll-out of cuts means that relative child poverty may increase to a new high of 37 per cent by 2023/24.

Of course, there is still much more we need to do to improve the quality and security of work, and maintain recent stronger pay growth. But entering work remains a key route out of poverty, as Figure 4.5 shows. A child living in poverty in 2016/17 had a 45 per cent chance of leaving poverty by the following year when a member of their household entered work, compared to only a 22 per cent chance of leaving poverty if their household remained workless. This increased to a 64 per cent chance if a second earner joined the workforce in a previously single-earner household in poverty.

Conclusion

Two lessons stand out from the 2010s for those concerned with reducing child poverty. First, our task is to secure strong economic and living standards growth to return to the reductions in absolute child poverty that we used to take for granted. That is easier said than done. But the second task is well within our reach: preventing reductions in state support from driving relative poverty up. In the decade ahead, it is time policy started to be part of the answer, not the problem.

Figure 4.5:

(Children have a better chance of getting out of poverty when someone in their household enters work, and the impact is greater if this is a second earner.)

Proportion of children in poverty in 2016/17 who left poverty in 2017/18, by change in number of workers in the household

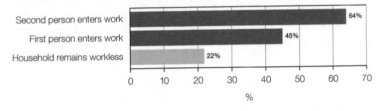

Notes: Dependent children only. Only includes households where the overall number of adults stays the same.

Source: Resolution Foundation analysis of Institute for Social and Economic Research, Understanding Society data

---

Notes and references

1   Absolute poverty: poverty measured against a fixed, rather than relative, real terms poverty line.

2   Predistribution: distribution resulting from market forces or economic growth.

3   A Corlett and others, *The Living Standards Audit 2019*, Resolution Foundation, 2019

4   A Corlett, *The Living Standards Outlook 2019*, Resolution Foundation, 2019

5   T Bell and L Gardiner, *Feel Poor, Work More: explaining the UK's record employment*, Resolution Foundation, 2019

6   G Bangham, *The Times They Aren't A-changin': why working hours have stopped falling in London and the UK*, Resolution Foundation, 2020

7   Calculations from the Policy Measures Database, Office for Budget Responsibility

8   F Rahman, *The Generation of Poverty: poverty over the life course for different generations*, Resolution Foundation, 2019

Five

Poverty, work and family: what has changed for lone mothers and their children since 2000?

Jane Millar and Tess Ridge

The 'end child poverty' pledge had special meaning for lone mothers. At the start of the twenty-first century, the financial position of the UK's estimated 1.7 million lone-parent families was generally bleak. This was the group with one of the highest risks of income poverty, less than half were employed and six in ten were receiving income support. These families were a key group if the 'end child poverty' target was to have any chance of success. And for the Labour government, the main route to ending child poverty was through employment. In November 2000 Gordon Brown, the Chancellor of the Exchequer, set another explicit and important target – 70 per cent of lone parents to be in employment by 2010. A range of policy provisions and measures were being put in place or expanded.[1]

We started our research on lone mothers and employment with a first round of interviews with 50 women early in 2004.[2] These women had left income support and started working in 2002/03. By that time, the New Deal for Lone Parents was well established, benefits for children had been increased and the tax credits system offered higher levels of ongoing financial support. This included some support for childcare costs. The policy environment was thus supportive, possibly more so than before or since.

This was reflected in our first round of interviews, where there was generally a positive feeling. At that time, there was no compulsion on lone parents to seek work, regardless of the age of their children. So starting work was their own decision, often supported – both emotionally and practically – by their families, in particular by their children and their parents. But the support they received from the government was also crucial. Almost all had had help from the New Deal programme, and were often very positive about their personal advisers, who smoothed the path into work with, for example, benefit run-ons, help with work-related costs, and help with claiming in-work tax credits. The tax credits themselves were an extremely important component of family income, topping up low wages to a level that enabled the families to feel a bit better off in work than they had been before.

Not all was perfect of course. It was challenging to maintain work and care for their children. Steady jobs were hard to find and, as a result, there was a lot of job changing and movement between jobs. The tax credits could be erratic and unreliable, and repaying overpayments was a challenge. There were still debts to be paid, and money was often tight. Not everyone was able to sustain work, particularly when jobs were temporary, or when there were health issues.

However, fast forward to our final interviews with 15 of the families in 2016,[3] the policy environment by then was very different, not just for lone mothers but in general for people with low incomes. The focus on employment was still central, but now the system was now more focused on compulsion than support. The work conditionality requirements and sanctions were tougher, with lone parents with children aged three and above required to be available for, and actively seeking, work. The labour market was more challenging. Jobs were available, but insecure and temporary work was more common. The specialist New Deal programmes were gone. The system of tax credits was being replaced by universal credit, and ongoing 'austerity' cuts to benefits were hitting families with children and young people particularly hard. On the positive side, the childcare offer for three- and four-year-olds had been expanded, but still with gaps in affordable provision especially for school-age children.

Two things stood out for us as we analysed the 2016 data and compared this with earlier rounds of the research. First, the employment trajectories over time for the women showed strong commitment of the mothers to staying in work. Most had continued to work, with various job changes along the way, but it was clearly difficult to achieve in-work progression and advancement. The wages of the women did not change much in real terms over time. For some families, this meant living on a low income over a period of years, not least as tax credits ended when children grew up. For others, wages did increase but this in itself did not necessarily translate into security. Events that can happen to anyone – poor health, children leaving home, unemployment, accidents and so on – are particularly challenging for people without many resources to fall back on.

Second, it was a real challenge for the young people – who were in their late teens or early twenties by 2016 – to establish themselves in the adult world. They were seeking to study, to start work, to leave home and to become independent in the context of a largely unsupported, indeed often hostile, policy environment. Young people's transitions into training and employment were often fragile and influenced by financial insecurity, housing instability and precariousness in employment. Support from the state was severely limited, following the removal of advice and support services for young people such as Connexions and the education mainte- nance allowance (in England). These disadvantages were coupled with benefit provisions that are often lower and more restrictive for young peo- ple than for adults. The mothers were able to help to some extent but were limited by their own lack of resources.

What lessons can we learn?

The employment rates of lone mothers are now at 70 per cent,[4] meeting the target set in 2000. Policy can therefore start at a different point – it need not be all about getting people into work. We can start to think in a more granular way now.

Those lone mothers not working include some specific groups, in particular mothers with very young children, with large families and with health issues. There will also be some women who have recently become lone mothers, who will be trying to stabilise their families and establish themselves, sometimes after moving home. This is even more challenging in cases where domestic violence is involved. Finding a job may not be an immediate priority, or the best thing, for them and their families. Adequate support while not working – one of the original aims of any social security system – is necessary. And, for those who do want to start work, the approach of the New Deal for Lone Parents would offer more appropriate support than the more punitive work requirements in universal credit.

Those lone mothers in work also require ongoing financial support. Universal credit needs significant reform in order to provide a more stable and secure source of income. This would mean changes to aspects of the design to ensure that recipients receive their full entitlements in a timely way. It would also mean looking at how to restore, or improve, the value of universal credit, reduced by the benefit freeze and other cuts. Families with children, including lone parents, have (as other chapters in the book also cover) borne much of the weight of these cuts, and this should be reversed if the government is serious about the end of austerity.

Support for young people also needs a radical rethink. This is a group that seems to have fallen off the radar over the past 20 years, and provision is woefully inadequate both in the type and level of support.

There seems to be no coherent view of what is needed, of what families can and cannot do, and of where additional measures are needed. Clear rethinking and seeking consensus around the issue of support for young people needs to be a priority.

Let's leave the final word with one of our young people, reflecting on the challenges of growing up in a working, but low-income, lone-parent family.

> 'I guess growing up I have realised that, wow, it must have been hard for my mum, and she still, you know, achieved a lot, done a lot. But it's hard for me as well to progress because I don't have the – you could say – but I guess it's – I don't want to say it's all financial, but there is a big – it is quite – it is all financial, really. I suppose if we all had a lot of money then lives would be a lot easier.'

Over the years, this research has been funded by the Economic and Social Research Council (RES-000-23-1079), by the Department of Work and Pensions, and by the Joseph Rowntree Foundation.

Notes and references

1   J Millar, 'Work as welfare? Lone mothers, social security and employment', in P Saunders, *Welfare to Work in Practice: social security and participation in economic and social life*, Ashgate Publishing, 2005

2   T Ridge and J Millar, *Work and Well-being Over Time: lone mothers and their children*, Department for Work and Pensions Research Report No.536, 2008

3   J Millar and T Ridge, *Work and Relationships Over Time in Lone-mother Families*, Joseph Rowntree Foundation, 2017

4   Office for National Statistics, *Families and the Labour Market, UK: 2019*, October 2019

Six

What needs to happen to financial support for children?

Mike Brewer

In March 1999, as a junior economist in HM Treasury, I began a stint in the team that focused on poverty analysis, social security reform and work incentives. I was looking forward to it being a little quieter than my previous position working on tax policy and editing Budget documents. Well, it was a nice idea! By the end of my first week, it felt like every senior official had responded to Tony Blair's Toynbee Hall speech by asking for a briefing on what child poverty was, and how it could be reduced. With typical Treasury directness, one question was 'how generous would we need to make the Working Families' Tax Credit to ensure no family in work would be in poverty?'.

'Rather a lot' was the gist of my (no doubt very precisely calculated) reply, and this is one reason why the relative measures of child poverty never fell as low as the hoped-for 5 or even 10 per cent. But it underlines that financial support for children was always at the core of the 1997–2010 Labour government's drive to reduce child poverty. Although the initial drive behind Treasury reforms was to make work pay, the priority quickly changed to being about supporting families, with HM Treasury in 1999 describing its approach as one that would 'provide direct financial support to all families recognising the extra costs of children'. The subsequent policy measures from the Labour government were a comprehensive assault on child poverty regardless of parental employment status.

In analysis in 2010, with then colleagues of mine at the Institute for Fiscal Studies, we showed conclusively that the way that families with children are supported through the tax and benefit system had a 'very strong influence' on measures of child poverty. We showed that:[1]

> direct tax and benefit policy [...] plays an important role in explaining at least three things: the large overall reduction in child poverty since 1998–99; the striking slowdown in progress towards the child poverty targets between 2004–05 and 2007–08; and some of the variation in child poverty trends between different groups of children.

Of course, with an income-based poverty measure, it is not surprising that money matters. But this was a period where employment trends were particularly favourable, and even then we still attributed only a small amount of the poverty changes to the labour market (of the fall in child poverty of 3.9 percentage points between 1998 and 2008, only 0.7 percentage points could be linked to changes in the work patterns of parents). So financial support for children really is crucial to determining child poverty trends.

Our work also showed that policy changes under the Labour government had not simply moved children from just below to just above an arbitrary poverty line: instead, policy changes allowed the bottom – generally defined – to catch up with the middle – generally defined. Relative poverty would have fallen by just as much for any relative poverty lines from 50 per cent to 70 per cent of median income (with child poverty falling the most for a poverty line set at 65 per cent of median income).

Ten years later, and the picture for child poverty and financial support for children is much less optimistic. Families with children bore the brunt of the austerity-induced cuts to social security, first to tax credits for families with children and then to universal credit. The familiar Institute for Fiscal Studies (IFS) analysis after each Budget shows a clear picture where, at each level of income, cuts to financial support since 2010 have fallen the most heavily on families with children compared with working-age adults without children, and especially compared with those of pension age, who have tended to gain from generous over-indexation of state pensions. One of the most damaging changes – if you have child poverty in mind – was the two-child limit to tax credits and universal credit. In 2009, I showed that an increase in financial support for large families would be a very well-targeted measure for reducing child poverty. It was not a surprise, therefore, to find out that a reform that focused cuts on large families would have such a dramatic impact on child poverty numbers.

To conclude, making serious inroads into child poverty means considering the way in which the whole tax and benefit system supports families with children, and means thinking sensibly about rates and generosity now and in future. Even though universal credit arguably makes it easier to do just that, it seems many years since we have had a full debate about the structure and generosity of financial support for children. Politicians have focused first on austerity-driven cuts to social security programmes, and then have been distracted by the implementation and operational issues of universal credit. Campaigners have, arguably, been fighting battles one cut at a time. If we are to make a long-term plan for reducing child poverty, then, unsurprisingly, at the top of the list should be undoing the two-child limit. We should also look closely at measures that affect certain vulnerable groups disproportionately, like the lower rate of universal credit for young parents, and the benefit cap. But we also need to return to the idea that benefit entitlements for families with children should be rising at least as fast as prices, and ideally by as much as median income. Without that, there is little hope of making sustained improvements to the numbers of children in poverty.

Notes and references

1   M Brewer and others, *Child Poverty in the UK Since 1998–99: lessons from the past decade*, IFS Working Paper 10/23, Institute for Fiscal Studies, 2010, available at ifs.org.uk/publications/ 5303

Seven

Measuring, monitoring and making progress: what targets should we have?

Jonathan Portes

One clear lesson from recent British political history is that targets matter, as long as politicians genuinely feel accountable for them, and that there is a price to be paid for failing to meet them. That impact can be benign, as with the child poverty target under New Labour; it can also be malign, both in policy terms and for the government, as with the Cameron/May target to reduce net immigration to the tens of thousands.

It is impossible to reduce issues like poverty to a single number or set of numbers. But without quantifiable measures and targets, it is too easy for politicians to get away with rhetoric, backed up with the occasional 'eye-catching initiative'. Previous experience with the child poverty target illustrates the point. As Fraser Nelson put it:

> At the heart of the Child Poverty Act lies an agenda which has arguably done more damage to Britain's social fabric than any idea in modern history. It is based on the Eurostat definition of poverty: an income 40 per cent below the national average... instead of fighting poverty, the Labour government spent billions manipulating a spreadsheet – to catastrophic effect.[1]

To put it simply, what Nelson was – correctly – saying, is that the 1997–2010 Labour government sought to reduce poverty by increasing the incomes of people who were poor, hence taking them out of poverty. And that in order to determine how to do that, HM Treasury and the Department for Work and Pensions (DWP) modelled the impact of different policy options on family incomes, and in turn on the child poverty target.

In this sense, policy – meaning how much the tax and benefit system should be used to redistribute income towards those on lower incomes – was indeed driven by targets and models. Without this apparatus, it is very difficult to see that the programme of redistribution – and hence the reductions in poverty that resulted – would have been feasible and sustainable.

So, while quantifiable targets of some sort are not sufficient – and indeed, as has been well documented, they can distort priorities and decision making in some circumstances – they are certainly necessary.

But few targets have been more contested than the child poverty target. Some reject the notion that we should define 'poverty' as anything other than lack of the basic means of survival, pointing to the conditions of the poor in developing countries, where many may lack access to basic sanitation, electricity or even enough food. While true, that is not a sensible way of thinking about poverty in the UK, and has not been since Adam Smith defined 'necessaries':

> By necessaries I understand not only the commodities which are indispensably necessary for the support of life, but what ever the customs of the country renders it indecent for creditable people, even the lowest order, to be without. A linen shirt, for example, is, strictly speaking, not a necessary of life. The Greeks and Romans lived, I suppose, very comfortably, though they had no linen. But in the present times, through the greater part of Europe, a creditable day-labourer would be ashamed to appear in public without a linen shirt, the want of which would be supposed to denote that disgraceful degree of poverty which, it is presumed, nobody can well fall into, without extreme bad conduct. Custom, in the same manner, has rendered leather shoes a necessary of life in England.[2]

A different line of attack came from Iain Duncan Smith and the Centre for Social Justice (CSJ), which argued that 'poverty is not just about income… poverty is a multifaceted phenomenon which cannot be eradicated without an acknowledgement of its key drivers: family breakdown, educational failure, economic dependency and worklessness, addiction and serious personal debt. These drivers diminish the future opportunities of a child and so must also be at the heart of any serious attempt to measure poverty.'[3]

On the face of it, this is either a tautology or a fallacy. Reducing poverty requires addressing the 'root causes'; equally obviously, factors like 'family breakdown', while they may or may not cause poverty, do not in themselves constitute poverty. My income may be a crude and imperfect measure of whether I can afford Adam Smith's 'necessaries'; the fact my parents are divorced, however, is not a measure at all.

So, many of us from what you might call the 'reality-based community' of poverty researchers were more than a little worried by the establishment of the Social Metrics Commission (SMC), under the chairmanship of Philippa Stroud, formerly head of the CSJ, with a remit 'to develop metrics that better reflect the nature and experiences of poverty that different families in the UK have.'[4]

We feared that the Commission would devise a measure that would downplay, or eliminate, the central role of income – which is what determines what an individual or family can or cannot afford – in favour, as the CSJ argued, of an amorphous set of indicators, like family structure, that were only indirectly under government control, and hence could easily be used by government to evade its responsibilities.

We were wrong. The Commission concluded unequivocally that access to financial resources was the central and fundamental measure of poverty:

> The Commission decided to focus its measure of poverty on the extent to which the material resources that someone has available to them now are sufficient to meet the material needs that they currently have.[5]

In practice, that meant that it recommended some broadly sensible adjustments to the current income measure (including a measure of easy access to financial assets, such as savings, and adjustments for the costs of disability) but retained the basic principle of the current measure – a poverty threshold set as a proportion of median household income. These changes, which are backed up by rigorous analysis, would attune the measure of relative income poverty more closely to the actual lived experience of individuals and families without enough income or savings to afford 'necessaries', at the cost of introducing a number of complex and necessarily subjective adjustments, making the measure less transparent and more subject to fine-tuning.

So, where does that leave the targets debate? In one sense, it is over; nobody with any credibility is any longer arguing that relative income poverty is not the central measure of poverty. If the choice is between the standard relative poverty measure that we have used for half a century, and that proposed by the Social Metrics Commission, this is a largely technical issue that should be left to nerds like me. I would favour sticking with the current suite of measures: they are simple, well established, there is a long time series of data and analysis based on them, and they are at least to some extent internationally comparable. But adopting the proposals of the SMC would – in contrast to the earlier ideas of the CSJ – be far from a disaster, and could drive a greater focus on people with disabilities, who are arguably ill served by the current measure, and to some extent on families with children. These would be welcome improvements. Overall, the arguments are fairly balanced: no one should spend too much time arguing over this issue.

But setting a target is only the first step. The first, and perhaps the most important, prerequisite for a successful cross-government strategy on any issue is political commitment and political leadership from the top. That may sound obvious. But it means more than a sound bite, or even a speech. Tony Blair's 1999 speech setting out the Labour government's objective of halving, and then eliminating, child poverty, did genuinely drive policy, particularly in the Treasury and DWP.

But it is worth examining why it did so. Most importantly, it was not just a speech, and it was not just Blair. Blair and Gordon Brown were genuinely committed to this goal politically; and No.10 and the Treasury were committed institutionally. This meant that even many years after the speech itself had been made, and the specific words largely forgotten, the ultimate objective was still driving policy.

If you think a particular set of issues is important, not just in respect of a limited set of policies, but across government, and you want Ministers and civil servants to take account of those issues whenever they are making policy, then an obvious approach is to force them to do so.

But there are downsides to targets – any targets. They drive a focus on measures that have a direct, short-term, and quantifiable impact on the target, whatever it is. Sometimes that focuses minds, but it can also distort policy. Many policy measures have impacts that are hard to quantify; and even when they can be quantified, numbers alone are rarely enough to judge impact, particularly on contested concepts like poverty and social justice, and over the longer term. So, a broader perspective is required – not just spreadsheets – but that does not mean that rigorous and objective analysis is either impossible or unnecessary.

This is underlined by the increasingly important imperative to consider intersectionality, or how impacts and outcomes differ not just on one dimension but multiple dimensions. In the context of poverty, it is hardly sensible to ignore the fact that the impact of a policy designed to improve the opportunities of people with disabilities cannot just focus on the impact on people with disabilities on average, but must also consider gender, ethnicity and socioeconomic status. But any quantitative analysis quickly runs into the problem that there are literally thousands of possible subgroups: analysing them all, even if data permitted – which it usually does not – is not a viable way of evaluating the impact of policy.

So what actions, structures and resources would be required to reflect these principles in order to support a genuinely transformative government focus on child poverty? I would propose something like the following:

- A clear political commitment, enshrined in law, from the Prime Minister to specific, measurable objectives to reduce poverty and inequality.

- The Act would establish a new, independent body, building on the Social Mobility Commission but structured much more like the Office for Budget Responsibility (OBR). It would be located within the Cabinet Office, which would host and fund its secretariat, but like the OBR would have only independent members, appointed by government on the basis of a transparent selection process and approved by parliament. Like the OBR but unlike the SMC, members would all be selected for their expertise.

- The Act would set out a mandate to the new body, analogous to that of the OBR, to report to parliament (annually or semi-annually) on whether the government's policies, taken as a whole, were likely to achieve the government's objectives on poverty and inequality, including any specific targets (such as the Child Poverty target). These reports would include the type of analysis described above, include cumulative impact assessments across a number of dimensions. In addition, there would be regular analytic reports on the very long-term impacts of policy on inequality and poverty.

- It would have its own dedicated analytical capacity (some of which, in particular in the area of simulating the impact of changes to taxes and benefits might be shared with the OBR). It would also, like the OBR have the ability to commission bespoke analysis from HM Treasury, DWP and others.

None of this institutional and structural change is remotely a substitute for actual policies – changes to taxes and benefits, new programmes and policies. But equally, without a degree of central direction, co-ordination, analysis and monitoring, the momentum generated by individual policies, however good, will be lost.

Notes and references

1   J Portes, 'The contradictions of Fraser Nelson', April 2017, http://notthetreasuryview. blogspot.com/2017/04

2   M Thoma, 'Adam Smith on relative poverty', 28 March 2006, https://economistsview. typepad.com

3   Centre for Social Justice, *Rethinking Child Poverty*, 2012

4   https://socialmetricscommission.org.uk

5   Social Metrics Commission, *A New Measure of Poverty for the UK: a summary of the report by the Social Metrics Commission*, September 2018

Eight

'Everyone's expecting me to fail': children's and families' experiences of poverty

Gill Main

Over the past two decades we have heard a lot about children and families living in poverty. The focus of this attention has shifted from a strong political will to end child poverty, promised in Tony Blair's 1999 speech and enshrined in the 2010 Child Poverty Act, to an approach of disregarding and denying the very existence of child poverty,[1] evidenced in the repeal of the 2010 Act in the 2016 Welfare Reform and Work Act, and dismissive responses[2] to the 2018 United Nations (UN) Special Rapporteur's report[3] which demonstrated that poverty in the UK is a serious problem and a political choice. Commentary on the prevalence and nature of poverty is ubiquitous, but with varying and all too often minimal consideration of evidence in how poverty, and people living in poverty, are portrayed.

What is notable by its absence is the knowledge of people with direct experience of poverty. In particular, it is rare that children in poverty are given the opportunity to tell their stories and have their say in interventions, or in how their lives are portrayed. The stigma of poverty means that adults in poverty are often silenced;[4] the stigma of poverty coupled with societal views about childhood means that children are doubly so. This is problematic for multiple reasons. Academic evidence shows us that children in poverty are often very aware of their family's financial situation and the negative impact this has on their lives.[5] Unless we listen to children directly, we cannot fully understand how, when and why poverty harms them.[6] Legally, the UN Convention on the Rights of the Child 1989 is underpinned by the principle – enshrined in Article 12 and agreed upon as an overarching consideration in interpreting the Convention as a whole[7] – that children should be listened to and their views taken seriously in issues affecting them. It would be difficult to argue that child poverty, which blights wellbeing during childhood and across the life course,[8] does not constitute a matter that affects children.

A programme of research led at the University of Leeds, conducted in partnership with the Child Poverty Action Group, Leeds City Council, and The Children's Society, aims to address the absence of children's and families' knowledge in how child poverty is understood and measured. This research has drawn on a wide range of approaches including focus groups, interviews, ethnography, surveys and participatory research, with the aim of centralising the expertise of children, young people and families with lived experience of poverty in how poverty is understood and acted upon. Over the course of nearly a decade, new measures, models and resources have been produced which have begun to influence academic, policy and practice approaches to child poverty. Here, some of the key messages from the people who have contributed their time and expertise are summarised.

1 Parents living in poverty are doing their very best for their children

Much of what we hear about families in poverty from politicians and the media focuses on the behaviours and attitudes of parents. They are portrayed as prioritising their own (maybe illicit) wants over their children's needs, as less skilled (in parenting, work, and life) than better-off parents, and as requiring external, often state-supplied, motivation to earn money to support their families.[9] Yet qualitative and quantitative evidence shows us that parents in low-income households often go to extreme lengths to provide for their children, going without basic necessities such as enough to eat in order that their children do not go hungry;[10] that the aspirations parents hold for their children do not differ across families at different levels of income, but rather that the resources parents can plough into extracurricular opportunities differ;[11] and that the vast majority of children in poverty live in households with at least one adult in paid work,[12] with many parents reporting holding down multiple jobs and working excessive hours just to get by.[13] This indicates that better financial support and infrastructure (such as adequate transport to work and good working conditions) are needed, rather than changes in the attitudes of parents.

2 Children living in poverty are doing their very best for their families

Parenting in poverty requires great sacrifice, as noted above, on the part of parents. But it is not possible for parents to shield children entirely from the reality of their situation,[14] and neither is it necessarily desirable: Main and Mahony[15] found that children who have a better knowledge of their household's financial situation are often happier overall and in their relationships with their parents than those who do not have such knowledge. Indeed, just as parents will hide their own needs from other family members to save money and reduce stress on tight budgets, so too do children and young people adopt active, self-sacrificing means of promoting personal and family survival. Many young people seek employment – formal or otherwise – to earn money to support their families.[16] Children from low-income households are substantially more likely to have pretended they do not wish to have, or do, something which costs money to save their family money; they are also 5.5 times more likely than non-poor children to have gone hungry because there was not enough money for food.[17] This confirms the importance of listening to children directly, and providing non-judgemental support to families in understanding how they manage meagre resources.

3 Families in poverty are not behaving differently to better-off families

Common responses to child poverty include interventions like parenting skills programmes and financial management courses. While all parents should be supported to gain the skills they need to parent and budget effectively, the targeting of such interventions at families in poverty would suggest that these families are behaving differently in how they use their resources compared to better-off families. In reality, studies of parenting[18] and of family resource sharing[19] demonstrate that there are overwhelming similarities in how families in poverty parent and share resources compared to better-off families, and that differences which are found often result from the intolerable stress which poverty presents. This indicates that a financial, rather than a behavioural, intervention is necessary if the intention of policy is to improve the lives of children and families.

4 Negative media and policy rhetoric harms children and families

Common assumptions about the nature of childhood and the role of children in society would suggest that children are not exposed to the harm that negative stereotypes in policy and in the media can do. These assumptions are challenged by the fact that research detailed above demonstrates that children are often much more aware of their family's financial situation than the adults around them know. Children's awareness, however, goes beyond family finances and includes an awareness of the pejorative stereotypes associated with poverty, and with receiving state or charitable support. Research with children as young as eight has shown that they have a strong awareness of who among their peers has less, and engage in bullying and exclusionary behaviours towards poorer peers.[20] In secondary schools, children in poverty report being bullied for their lack of resources, not only by peers but also by teachers and other adults in school, including being made to take smaller portions at lunch because they receive free school meals.[21] Permitting hostile media reports and policy rhetoric creates an atmosphere within which such bullying and exclusion is not only tolerated but encouraged – and children in poverty are the people who suffer because of this. To say that this is not the hallmark of a civilised or decent society is an understatement.

5 Children, young people and parents know what needs to be done

Finally, however, there is good news – children, young people and parents with lived experience of poverty can tell us what needs to change, and have ideas about what can be done to create a just society. Participatory research conducted with diverse groups of children, young people and parents in Leeds and London provide remarkably similar recommendations – all embedded in local communities so that the change required is concrete and feasible.[22] People want safe places to live, free from the fear of crime and with police forces they can trust. They want good educational opportunities for children and good employment opportunities for parents. They want affordable and accessible services like doctors, job centres and careers advisers. They want to be paid fairly for work and to be able to rely on an adequate safety net when things go wrong. They want houses which are well maintained and which do not pose a threat to their health. They want accountability in how the media and politicians talk about them. This list of demands is hardly excessive or complicated.

Poverty is often presented as a difficult problem to solve. Certainly, it has plagued societies for centuries with countless losses to human potential. But in the world's sixth largest economy, there can be no excuse for the extent and levels of poverty which we see in the UK today. Perhaps by listening to children and young people, who can tell us exactly what we should be doing to create a society in which everyone has the resources they need, we can begin to reverse the trend of the past decade.

Notes and references

1   P Butler, 'Tory peer says poor people go hungry because they do not know how to cook', *The Guardian*, 8 December 2014

2   R Booth, 'UN poverty expert hits back over UK minister's "denial of facts"', *The Guardian*, 24 May 2019

3   Office of the High Commission on Human Rights, 'Statement on visit to the United Kingdom, by Professor Philip Alston, United Nations Special Rapporteur on extreme poverty and human rights', 16 November 2018

4   R Walker, *The Shame of Poverty*, Oxford Scholarship Online, 2014

5   T Ridge, *Childhood Poverty and Social Exclusion: from a child's perspective*, Policy Press, 2002

6   G Main and S Mahony, *Fair Shares and Families: rhetoric and reality in the lives of children and families in poverty*, The Children's Society, 2018

7   Child Rights Connect, 'Key children's rights principles to underpin a UN Human Rights Council resolution on the Protection of the Rights of the Child in Humanitarian Situations', ohchr.org/Documents/Issues/Children/HumanitarianSituations/ChildRightsConnect.pdf

8   J Bradshaw, *The Well-being of Children in the UK*, Policy Press, 2016

9   Department for Work and Pensions and Department for Education, *A New Approach to Child Poverty: tackling the causes of disadvantage and transforming families' lives*, Cm 8061, 2011

10 G Main and J Bradshaw, 'Child poverty in the UK: measures, prevalence and intra-household sharing', *Critical Social Policy*, 36(1), 2016, pp38–61

11 G Main and S Mahony, *Fair Shares and Families: rhetoric and reality in the lives of children and families in poverty*, The Children's Society, 2018

12 Department for Work and Pensions, *Households Below Average Income: an analysis of UK income distribution, 1994/95–2017/18*, 2019

13 A Different Take London Panel, CPAG and University of Leeds, *Pushing Back: our take on life in poverty in London*, October 2019

14 T Ridge, *Childhood Poverty and Social Exclusion*, Policy Press, 2002

15 G Main and S Mahony, *Fair Shares and Families: rhetoric and reality in the lives of children and families in poverty*, The Children's Society, 2018

16 G Main and others, *More Snakes than Ladders: a report from the A Different Take Leeds panel*, University of Leeds and Leeds City Council, 2019

17 G Main and S Mahony, *Fair Shares and Families: rhetoric and reality in the lives of children

and families in poverty, The Children's Society, 2018

18 E Dermott and M Pomati, '"Good' parenting" practices: how important are poverty, education and time pressure?', *Sociology*, 50(1), 2016, pp125–142

19 G Main and S Mahony, *Fair Shares and Families: rhetoric and reality in the lives of children and families in poverty*, The Children's Society, 2018

20 G Main, *A Child-Derived Material Deprivation Index*, 2013. Unpublished PhD thesis submitted to the University of York in September 2013

21 A Different Take London Panel, CPAG and University of Leeds, *Pushing Back: our take on life in poverty in London*, October 2019

22 A Different Take London Panel, CPAG and University of Leeds, *Pushing Back: our take on life in poverty in London*, October 2019; G Main and others, *More Snakes than Ladders: a report from the A Different Take Leeds panel*, University of Leeds and Leeds City Council, 2019

Nine

Harnessing all the expert knowledge to understand poverty in all its forms and to identify what must change

Paul Dornan and Diana Skelton

'Today it is heartbreaking to see how divided our nation has become. It is high time to reclaim peace and solidarity between communities. People in poverty feel they are treated as less than human, which fuels a cycle of fury, anger, and rejection. Many of our public policies concerning Universal Credit, health care and housing actively harm people, even to the point of causing their death.' (Moraene Roberts, anti-poverty campaigner)[1]

What is poverty today and who gets to decide what matters most? These key questions are central to a new global research study into poverty in all of its forms published by All Together in Dignity / ATD Fourth World and the University of Oxford in 2019.[2] The UK was part of the study, along with Bangladesh, Bolivia, France, Tanzania and the United States, and the findings will help us when it comes to devising any future poverty strategy. This chapter outlines the results of the UK study. While this study was focused on working-age adults, many themes came out which were also relevant for child poverty. Moraene was a leading member of the research group that led the UK study and was due to co-author this chapter but died before this was possible. Her passion and wisdom guided the research through its many challenging stages. She will be sorely missed by all who knew her.

Moraene described her experience of poverty this way: 'I was born into poverty, came out of it a bit through regular work, and fell back into poverty as a young mum when I got divorced. It's what I live and it's what I fight' against. Her quotation at the top of this chapter reflects the harsh realities described by other people in poverty who took part in *Understanding Poverty in All its Forms: a participatory study into poverty in the UK*.[3] This chapter presents the results.

The study was designed to challenge traditional top-down approaches to research and public policy. People with lived experience of poverty are often the subjects of research analysed by others, an approach that is not rights based and deprives society of the knowledge of people in poverty. This study was different: participatory approaches were used to actively engage the knowledge and experience of people in poverty, as researchers as well as research participants. The study was also unique in bringing together different types of knowledge – from lived experience, as well as knowledge gained through professional work. Both types of knowledge are important and are more powerful in combination.

Focus groups took place in 2018 in the central belt in Scotland, and the South East and North of England. Thirteen groups met, often several times, to reflect together on the nature of poverty. The groups used not only discussion but also hands-on workshops that facilitated communication for those being asked for the first time to express their opinions in public. To achieve proper participation required building strong relationships, supported by spending time together for meals as much as in meetings. Half of these groups had a lived experience of poverty, and half had experience learned through their work as practitioners and professionals (such as those working in the public services), opinion formers and decision makers (including academics and journalists). Throughout, the research was led by a group of co-researchers who themselves had knowledge either through lived experience or from their work lives. It is this group which oversaw the research and was responsible for the findings. Details of the findings and methodology are available in *Understanding Poverty in All its Forms*.[4] The research documented six dimensions of poverty in the UK, which ought to be considered in any future strategy.[5]

- **Disempowering systems, structures and policies.** Economic, political and social structures can cause poverty. Policy is operated in a way that disempowers. Systems designed to support people are not working in ways that people want. Systemic cuts in funds for needed services have exacerbated inequality.

  'Poverty means being part of a system that leaves you waiting indefinitely in a state of fear and uncertainty.' (a participant with lived experience of poverty from the North of England)

- **Financial insecurity, financial exclusion and debt.** Financial insecurity means not being able to satisfy your basic needs. Worrying about money every day causes huge stress and misery.

'Poverty is worrying about money all of the time.' (a participant from a professional/practitioner group from the South East of England)

- **Damaged health and well-being.** Poverty is bad for health and can shorten life. It has a negative impact on physical, emotional, mental and social wellbeing.

  'Poverty is not being able to smell the flowers because the stress of life gets in the way.' (a participant with lived experience of poverty from the North of England)

- **Stigma, blame and judgement.** Misrepresentation about poverty in the UK and a lack of understanding lead to negative judgement, stigma and blame, which are deeply destructive to individuals and families. Prejudice and discrimination result in people in poverty feeling they are treated like lesser human beings.

  'Being in poverty makes you feel ashamed.' (a participant with lived experience of poverty from the North of England)

- **Lack of control over choices.** Poverty means a lack of control over choices and opportunities. Over time this can lead to increased social isolation and risk, as well as restricting people's social, educational and cultural potential. The lack of good options reduces people's control over their lives and traps people in repetitive cycles of hardship, disappointment and powerlessness. Lack of opportunity and choice increases risk and restricts options. Poverty is dehumanising. Moraene Roberts, presenting the research findings at the OECD in May 2019, said:

  'Poverty can limit joy, dreams and aspirations. We are not suggesting any intrinsic lack of aspirations among people living in poverty; but rather that poverty has a corrosive effect on people's sense of control over their lives. This theme was captured by statements such as: "Poverty means you are not allowed to be happy", or "I'm not able to smell the flowers because the stress of life gets in the way". Poverty can make people "afraid to dream". It "kills dreams and cages the dreamers".'

- **Unrecognised struggles, skills and contributions.** Too often, public discourse undervalues the contributions that people in poverty make to society while facing the daily impact of poverty. In addition to showing the damage poverty does, the co-researchers agreed that it was also crucial to show the active role of individuals experiencing poverty. These actions – such as budgeting or caring for others – demonstrate active resistance. These actions seldom come out in traditional research about poverty. The wealth of experience and life skills people in poverty possess is not recognised enough. Downplaying these actions fuels the painful judgement that people in poverty face.

> 'People in poverty are not passive victims. The research highlights how many people in poverty were making contributions and working hard in the face of difficulty. Ignoring their contributions fuels negative stereotypes.' (Moraene Roberts)

Recognising this resistance and hard work does not absolve policy makers from the need to act. Individual resilience is no substitute for better systems, structures and policies.

So, what needs to change in the UK in 2020?

Reflecting on the research, the co-researchers developed key messages including points about the human voice, disempowering systems and transformation. These messages should be central to developing a future strategy to tackle child poverty.

First, lack of money is central to poverty and so improving incomes needs to be central to tackling poverty. But there was also consensus that poverty goes beyond money to a lack of control, stigma, negative judgement, blame – and the devastating injustice of lives cut short. Co-researchers concluded that the human voice must not be lost to humanise the impact of poverty and build the case for greater action to tackle poverty.

Second, participants placed disempowering systems, structures and policies at the heart of the experience of poverty. Many policies and services are experienced in terms of stigma, judgement and control. Policy ought not to reinforce the lack of control people in poverty already experience. Concerns about stigma, judgement and control came out strongly in this research and much more so than in many studies which do not take this participatory approach. This importance of overcoming stigma, judgement and increasing individual control must be reflected in any future strategy.

Third, this study shows the transformative power of people in poverty playing key roles to build better understanding and reinforces the right to be heard. People in poverty, working with others on a level playing field, need to be fully and meaningfully involved in the development of policy responses to poverty. Achieving genuine participation is not easy – we had to work hard to get this right and there was scepticism that this could be another paper exercise. But achieving genuine participation can be a real driver of better knowledge and real change. Susan McMahon, one of the co-researchers, showed this, reflecting on her experience from the podium at the launch of the report:

> 'Doing this research woke me up to what was in me: the emotional crushed-ness that was inside me, a lot of blame, shame, guilt. If you are just struggling on every day you don't see any hope, then that's how you'll stay. But for me, my awakening sparked a change. I'm no longer crouched; I'm no longer crushed; I'm standing up.'

Moraene Roberts' conclusion echos Susan's belief that change is possible:

> 'It is a human right for each and every person to really live, not just to scrape by in misery. Society has to decide what we want to build in place of poverty. Our research findings, which come from the lived experience of many people in poverty, can help society change things so that human rights will once again become a tool for peace that belongs to everyone. Our experience, having come from very different backgrounds to lead this research together, shows what is possible when we aspire to challenge injustice. Today, we have a new opportunity to build the human connections that are so neces-sary for our society to overcome the violence of poverty.'

Notes and references

1   This is the title used by Moraene in ATD Fourth World, *The Roles We Play: recognising the contribution of people in poverty*, 2014
2   ATD Fourth World and the University of Oxford, *The Hidden Dimensions of Poverty: inter-national participatory research*, 2019
3   ATD Fourth World, *Understanding Poverty in All its Forms: a participatory research study into poverty in the UK*, 2019
4   See note 3.
5   Note that the text describing the dimensions of poverty draws heavily on the research report. The original text was agreed collectively by the co-researchers who led the UK study (see ATD Fourth World, *Understanding Poverty in All its Forms: a participatory research study into poverty in the UK*, 2019).

Ten

Understanding and responding to ethnic minority child poverty

Omar Khan

Rising child poverty in Britain is a serious problem, made more serious by the failure to understand why those numbers are growing and to focus on the right solutions to it. As with most policy areas, we need the right analysis to get the right solutions. So getting our analysis right is not just about winning an argument, but about reducing the numbers of children growing up in poverty, unable to afford adequate nutrition or a winter coat, or to realise their potential.

One particular area where our analysis is poor is ethnicity. Here too there is a wider point: the public and policy makers seem not to understand the nature and extent of racial inequalities in Britain in 2020, nor seem to be considering why those inequalities persist, still less what might be done to respond to them.

These may seem bold claims. Yet in terms of both analysis and policy, it is difficult to avoid the conclusion that ethnic minority child poverty is simply viewed as a non-issue. Taking analysis first: not only are the facts of ethnic minority child poverty shocking, they typically come as a shock or surprise. Around 60 per cent of Bangladeshi children, 54 per cent of Pakistani children and 47 per cent of black children are living in poverty (once housing costs are taken into account). However there is almost no public discussion or awareness of the extent of this poverty, and no policies formulated to address these stark numbers.

Consider also other policy areas, for example serious youth violence or safeguarding. Very little of the very public discussion on these issues addresses these stark levels of child poverty among ethnic minority people, nor much in the way of a response to that poverty. Furthermore, there is evidence that policy makers are going backwards in their understanding of child poverty and ethnicity.

A good (although hardly the only) example is the Troubled Families programme and the related efforts to define poverty (and child poverty) in

Table 10.1:

Child poverty* rate by ethnicity, before and after housing costs

Ethnic group	Poverty rate before housing costs	Poverty rate after housing costs
White	17	26
Mixed/multiple ethnic groups	26	41
Asian/Asian British	32	42
Indian	20	27
Pakistani	46	54
Bangladeshi	42	60
Chinese	22	31
Any other Asian background	23	41
Other ethnic group	33	53
Black/African/Caribbean/Black British	28	47
All children	19	30

Source: Department for Work and Pensions, *Households Below Average Income 1994/95–2017/18*, 2019, Table 4.5db

ways that downplay the role of income, while emphasising other factors, such as family breakdown, alcohol abuse and educational attainment. One consequence of this sort of policy thinking is that because Bangladeshi children are doing better in school, and because their parents are less likely to divorce or drink alcohol, the government may now view Bangladeshi children as being less likely to experience poverty, despite no change in their material circumstances.[1]

These examples highlight how ethnic minority child poverty is driven by factors that apply to all families living in poverty, as well as factors that are specific to ethnic minority households. One reason for higher child poverty among ethnic minority households is that such households are more likely to have certain demographic characteristics, for example having larger numbers of children or being relatively young, which increase the risk of poverty regardless of ethnicity.

Policy changes such as the benefit cap and the two-child limit have also led to a disproportionate increase in child poverty among ethnic minority children.[2] The government has neither denied these effects, nor proposed any mitigating measures, leading to the conclusion that it is satisfied that rising poverty among ethnic minority children is an acceptable consequence of its policy decisions.

The fact that half or more of some ethnic groups are growing up in poverty has widespread impact on their experience in schools and as young people. As the wider literature demonstrates, child poverty also has long-term 'scarring effects', meaning that those who experience child poverty have a greater risk of poor experiences as young adults, in middle age and as they age. In other words, the proven, widespread effects of child poverty on adults means that Britain will be living with the consequences of racial inequality into the 2100s (given that those born in, for example, 2012 are likely to live until their late eighties).

And it is not just the public or policy makers who do not always note the very high rates of ethnic minority child poverty. Even campaigners on child poverty often fail to mention the issue of race – for example, when highlighting those local areas with the highest child poverty. Agreement that rising child poverty requires a policy response may be widely agreed. However, the fact that the proportion of black and minority ethnic (BME) people in those areas is a major driver of rising child poverty is still too little discussed.

Of the top 17 local authorities with the highest rates of child poverty, 10 are in London, and listed in Table 10.2. In every one of these local authorities, BME children make up over half of the young population, rising to over 80 per cent in the two local authorities with the highest child poverty rates in the UK: Tower Hamlets and Newham. Among the non-London

Table 10.2:

Ten London local authorities with the highest child poverty rates

	% of 9–17 year olds who are BME	Child poverty rate
Tower Hamlets	80.9	56.7
Newham	81.8	51.8
Hackney	56.2	48.1
Islington	49.7	47.5
Westminster	56.1	46.2
Camden	49.4	43.5
Brent	72.7	43.1
Barking and Dagenham	59.3	42.8
Lambeth	62.6	42.8
Enfield	52.2	41.7

Sources: child poverty rates from J Stone and D Hirsch, *Local Indicators of Child Poverty, 2017/18: summary of estimates of child poverty in small areas of Great Britain*, End Child Poverty, 2019. The 9–17 year old BME population refers to 2019 data, projected from the 2011 census, where those children were 0–8 years old. We have not included 0–8 year olds in 2019 because the data for that group is less accurate at a local level for ethnic minorities, but they are likely to be even more diverse than their 9–17 year old peers.

local authorities with the highest child poverty, a similar pattern emerges: among children, Blackburn with Darwen (fifth highest child poverty rate in the country) is 46 per cent BME, Luton (seventh highest) is 65 per cent BME, and Manchester (eighth highest) is 52 per cent BME.

This leads to a wider point: that the focus on child poverty specifically (as contrasted with adult poverty), while understandable, can, however unintentionally, distract from some of the most important drivers of poverty in Britain's households. Children are poor because their parents are poor, and their parents are poor because they do not have enough money. It is obviously still sensible to focus on child poverty: because the effects are so widespread and longstanding, because any interventions in childhood are more likely to have consequential effects, because children are not yet fully moral agents or responsible for their choices, and because public opinion is more sympathetic to child poverty than it is to adult poverty.

So it certainly makes sense to focus on child poverty, and especially to ensure that early years interventions are effective as possible in reducing child poverty.[3] But ultimately the focus must expand beyond early years and schooling. Such interventions reduce the *consequential harm* of children living in poverty, but do not greatly reduce *the risk of* those children living in poverty in the first place (although they are likely to reduce the risk of the next generation of children being born into poverty).

The more general point is that 'child poverty' policy should focus on adult incomes. This should mean both expanding the social safety net and addressing structural inequalities in the labour market. It is now widely known that the majority of people living in poverty are in work,[4] and that the labour market is not always a route out of poverty. It is less commonly observed that the lower wages among many ethnic minority workers, combined with their greater likelihood of living in households with children (and their younger age profile), means that they are more likely to be affected by in-work poverty.

Given over five decades of evidence showing that ethnic minorities face discrimination in the labour market,[5] inequalities that result in greater rates of unemployment, under-employment (ie, working fewer hours or in less-qualified roles), as well as lower pay,[6] anyone who is serious about addressing ethnic minority child poverty, or indeed child poverty generally, needs to tackle discrimination.

The point could be extended further: policy makers and campaigners should focus on a wider range of policies that affect adults if they are going to effectively address child poverty. In addition to the labour market, housing is a major area where addressing costs would have a particularly beneficial effect for households living in poverty generally, and for ethnic minority households specifically. Ethnic minority households constitute fully half of overcrowded households in Britain (in many of which children are sharing bedrooms). The higher rates of 'after housing cost poverty' cited at the beginning of this chapter attest to the importance of addressing housing costs for tackling BME child poverty.

That half and more of black, Bangladeshi and Pakistani children are growing up in poverty in Britain in 2020 should be viewed as a national crisis, and should be getting much more policy concern. One speculative explanation for why these figures and the human lives behind them merit such little focus is that while children generally are viewed as more sympathetic and less blameworthy for their economic circumstances than adults, the public has less sympathy for ethnic minority children. Alternatively, rising poverty among ethnic minority children may be off the policy agenda because of the more general lack of focus on tackling racial inequalities – or indeed poverty or low pay – more broadly over the last decade.

Until we better understand the nature, causes and consequences of child poverty in Britain, we will be unlikely to effectively address that poverty. Among other groups, ethnic minority children have been particularly left behind by an analysis which fails to understand the reality of their experiences. This consequently means that we are not adequately grappling with the question of how we might better tackle ethnic minority child poverty in Britain. In this chapter, I have offered some suggestions for both how we might better understand ethnic minority child poverty, and how we might begin to address it.

Notes and references

1   See the Runnymede Trust's response to the Government's consultation on how to measure child poverty, 15 February 2012, https://www.runnymedetrust.org/uploads/Runnymede_ChildPovResponse%20(1).pdf

2   See, for example, O Khan, *The 2015 Budget: effects on Black and minority ethnic people*, Runnymede Trust, 2015

3   See, for example, the work of the Early Intervention Foundation, eif.org.uk

4   Joseph Rowntree Foundation, *UK Poverty 2019/20*, February 2020

5   See, for example, Di Stasio and Heath, *Are Employers in Britain Discriminating against Ethnic Minorities? Summary of findings from the GEMM project*, Centre for Social Investigation, Nuffield College, 2019; and M Wood and others, *A Test for Racial Discrimination in Recruitment Practice in British Cities*, Department for Work and Pensions Research Report No.607, 2009

6   Y Li and A Heath, 'Persistent disadvantages: a study of labour market dynamics of ethnic unemployment and earnings in the UK (2009–2015)', *Journal of Ethnic and Migration Studies*, 2018

Eleven

Eradicating child poverty: harder yet after Brexit?

Kitty Stewart

Here we are in 2020 and, far from being eradicated, child poverty is rising sharply. On top of this, the UK has formally left the European Union). These sentences read like a science fiction account of 2020 written from the safety of 1999; instead they are our reality. Does the decision to leave the EU have any likely bearing on trends in child poverty in the future? Will it make it easier or more difficult to end child poverty for good? The answer is discouraging: evidence suggests Brexit will create real additional challenges.[1] This means an even stronger commitment to ending child poverty is required.

There is a strong consensus that Brexit will have negative effects on the UK's economic growth, with greater impact the more distant the future trading and wider relationships between the UK and the EU. Lower growth will mean lower average living standards, although because effects are anticipated to be felt across the whole income distribution, only small effects have been predicted on relative poverty.[2] Nonetheless, there are several reasons for concern about the impact of the economic effects of Brexit on children living in poverty. First, higher inflation linked to currency depreciation will be felt more sharply in households that receive a higher share of their income in cash benefits – unless benefits keep pace with price increases. Post-Brexit inflation has already squeezed real incomes in households in receipt of benefits in the context of the cash freeze on working-age benefits.[3] The freeze comes to an end as planned in April 2020, with most working-age benefits rising in cash terms for the first time in five years, but at the time of writing, Boris Johnson's government has not yet set out its stall on uprating benefits going forward.

Second, slower growth will mean a smaller fiscal envelope and therefore less cash available both to increase benefit generosity and to invest in health, education, early years and children's social care. Children whose home circumstances are least able to shield and protect them will be those for whom reductions in public services will have most impact.

There are also likely to be differential regional and sectoral effects, due to differing exposures to EU trade. There is a striking overlap between the regions that have seen the greatest increases in child poverty in recent years and those predicted to be most at risk from economic effects of Brexit – the North East, Northern Ireland, the West Midlands, Wales and the North West.[4] Households starting in a more vulnerable position will find it hardest to adjust to new shocks. Not all analysts make the same predictions for regional impact; some place London and the South East at greatest risk because new trade barriers are likely to be greatest for services, especially financial services.[5] But these regions may well find it easiest to bounce back, as they did after the 2008 crisis, because of the size and diversity of the regional economy.

Aside from the broad economic effects, leaving the EU will bring about a series of further changes likely to affect children living in poverty. First, it looks fairly certain that the free movement of workers will come to an end. The evidence suggests that this is unlikely in itself to create additional employment opportunities or make a substantial difference to wages for UK born workers.[6] But it is likely to place additional pressure on the delivery of public services, exacerbating existing shortages in health and social care in particular, as EU migrants play an important role in these sectors.[7]

An end to free movement will particularly affect children with EU nationalities. If they are living in the UK already, these children are entitled to settled status but they are dependent on adults in their households to apply before the deadline. Children whose parents face language or disability-related barriers may be less likely to apply, while some parents may have greater difficulty in providing the evidence of residency required, including unpaid carers and those working cash in hand.[8] For EU children arriving in the future, access to social rights and entitlements including health care and social security may be at risk, depending on the immigration status of their parents and guardians.

Ending free movement will also make it more difficult and expensive for UK citizens to travel to the rest of the EU, as tourists (for whom visa and health insurance costs must now be considered) and to work and study. These opportunities were never equally shared across all young people; now more than ever they may become the preserve of richer families.

A further important change is that after Brexit the UK will no longer be subject to the Charter of Fundamental Rights enforced by the Court of Justice of the European Union. While the European Convention on Human Rights and the European Social Charter will still apply, the former does not cover social or economic rights, while the latter has no mechanism for judicial enforcement. It is argued that the UK will be left with a weakening of equality protection and important gaps in human rights protection, including the rights of the child.[9] Downward pressure on rights may be most likely in relation to employment protection. Children living with adults working part-time, long hours or as temporary or agency workers have all benefited from EU legislation that has enforced rights in the face of resistance from the UK government.[10] Matching EU employment protection may well be a condition of an extensive trade agreement with the EU, but in the absence of such an agreement these rights could be vulnerable given the need to secure wider trade deals and to attract investment to a UK outside the single market.

Finally, the UK will no longer be subject to the Open Method of Coordination (OMC) – the EU's mechanism of using the regular publication of social indicators to try to secure progress in social rights and to support the Europe 2020 targets for the reduction of the number of people living in poverty and material deprivation.[11] In practice, the OMC approach is argued to have made little real progress in reducing poverty, because the link between the indicators and policies has not been adequately articulated and trade-offs not made explicit.[12] Nonetheless, if the UK is dropped from Eurostat tables and maps, it will make it a bit more difficult to use an international perspective to hold the UK government to account.

While Brexit may add to the challenges of tackling poverty in the UK, it must not be used as an excuse not to take action. Indeed, it increases the imperative of developing a renewed anti-poverty strategy. This strategy should include steps to mitigate the potential impact of Brexit on more vulnerable groups, among them protecting the real value of cash benefits, investing in more disadvantaged regions (going further than replacing EU structural and investment funds), and committing to retaining employment protection legislation and to protecting the rights of the child. It should also include investment in further and higher education to widen opportunities for young people to develop careers in health and social care to help fill Brexit shortages. There is a key underlying problem: most of these steps require resources and Brexit will bring much tighter fiscal constraints. Regardless, the political will to prioritise action to eradicate child poverty must be found.

Notes and references

1   This chapter draws on analysis in K Stewart, K Cooper and I Shutes, *What Does Brexit Mean for Social Policy in the UK? An exploration of the potential consequences of the 2016 referendum for public services, inequalities and social rights*, Social Policy and Distributional Outcomes Research Paper 3, Centre for Analysis of Social Exclusion (CASE), 2019
2   H Barnard, L Heykoop and A Kumar, *How Could Brexit Affect Poverty in the UK?*, Joseph

Rowntree Foundation, 2018

3   H Breinlich and others, *The Brexit Vote, Inflation and UK Living Standards*, CEP Brexit Analysis No.11, Centre for Economic Performance, 2017; A Corlett, G Bangham and D Finch, *The Living Standards Outlook 2018*, Resolution Foundation, 2018

4   B Francis-Devine, L Booth and F McGuinness, *Poverty in the UK: statistics*, House of Commons Briefing Paper No.7096, 5 September 2019, on the regional differences in poverty 2015–2020; House of Commons Exiting the European Union Committee, *EU Exit Analysis Cross Whitehall Briefing*, January 2018

5   S Dhingra, S Machin and H Overman, 'Local economic effects of Brexit,' *National Institute Economic Review*, 242(1), 2017, ppR24–R36

6   S Nickell and J Salaheen, *The Impact of Immigration on Occupational Wages: evidence from Britain*, Bank of England Working Paper No.574, 2015; Migration Advisory Committee, *EEA Migration in the UK: final report*, 2018

7   See K Stewart, K Cooper and I Shutes (note 1 above) for discussion and references.

8   M Sumption and Z Kone, *Unsettled Status? Which EU citizens are at risk of failing to secure their rights after Brexit?*, Migration Observatory, University of Oxford, 2018

9   J Coppel QC, Legal opinion on European Union (Withdrawal) Bill – EU Charter of Fundamental Rights, commissioned by the Equality and Human Rights Commission, 2018; P Roderick and A Pollock, 'Brexit's Great Repeal Bill will axe the right to health', *British Medical Journal*, 357, 2017

10 M Ford, *'Workers' Rights from Europe: the impact of Brexit,* Independent legal opinion commissioned by the Trades Union Congress, 2016

11 B Cantillon, T Goedemé and J Hills (eds), 'Introduction', in *Decent Incomes for All: improving policies in Europe*, Oxford University Press, 2019

12 B Cantillon, T Goedemé and J Hills (eds), 'Introduction', in *Decent Incomes for All: improving policies in Europe*, Oxford University Press, 2019

Twelve

Sure Start, early childhood, education and care

Naomi Eisenstadt and Carey Oppenheim

It is now 21 years since Tessa Jowell announced the first 60 Sure Start trailblazer areas. These were to be the first of 250 local programmes located in low-income neighbourhoods. Each programme would combine childcare, health, family support and employment advice for all children under four and their families living in a defined catchment area. Alongside the ambitious Sure Start programme was a national childcare strategy to enable female employment, and a promise of 12.5 hours per week of early education for all four-year-olds during school terms. By 2001, this commitment of universal early education was expanded to include all three-year-olds. Up until 1997, the provision of services for families with children under five was left largely to local authorities. Some areas were very committed to providing a wide range of services for young children; other areas provided very little. Childcare was mainly provided by private and voluntary organisations. The local authority role was largely about young children who were deemed to be 'at risk'. While there were glimmers of progress prior to 1997, early childhood care and education became a key feature of public policy from that point onwards.

The basis for the early years interest was the wealth of evidence about the importance of this period of childhood to long-term child outcomes, as well as the damaging impact of living in poverty when very young. High-quality early education is associated with improved school readiness; starting school well is associated with improved results in the next stages of education. However, from the very beginning of new early years policies, there were tensions in the main aims: reducing the numbers of poor children by enabling female employment and ensuring poor children get the best start by offering childcare and early education that is both affordable and high quality.

Progress made

Unequivocally, good things have happened. Sure Start was cutting-edge, offering a holistic approach to families with young children and integrated services on one site. It was parent and community centred with a strong local voice. While the programme was initially designed for families living in poor areas, it was open to all, often enabling a social mix of children. Moreover, it became very popular. Service users loved it. However, the early evaluation results were mixed, showing that some groups were not benefiting from Sure Start. This led to modifications that significantly improved results. The most recent evidence shows that Sure Start, in its heyday, reduced hospitalisation among children aged 5–11 and was most effective in poor areas.[1] In 2002, Sure Start local programmes were rebadged as children's centres, and by 2004, a children's centre was promised for every neighbourhood in England, 3,500 in all. The childcare strategy was also showing results. Uptake of free hours of childcare was high. Women's employment, particularly of lone parents, increased substantially, in part because of the availability of childcare and childcare tax credits.[2] Child poverty was on the decline until 2004/05, mainly through generous tax credits for families and improvements in benefit rates. However, the gap in school readiness between poor children and their better-off peers remained stubbornly wide.

Another unequivocally good thing that began in 1997 and has continued under Coalition and Conservative governments has been improvements in maternity, paternity, parental leave and rights to flexible working. Paid maternity leave increased over the period from 16 weeks to nine months. Two weeks paid paternity leave was introduced and since 2010 there have been some steps to start to rectify the imbalance between women and men's entitlement, increasing the flexibility of leave between parents and extending the right to flexible working for all employees. However, fathers' take-up of their entitlements is still low. The emphasis on parental leave has in part been due to increasing interest and evidence about the importance for healthy brain development of early attachment for infants as well as the need to retain women in the workplace.

Reversals

But since 2010, much progress has been rolled back. On the positive side, free hours of childcare were extended to disadvantaged two-year-olds, but at the same time a series of changes to early years policy significantly weakened what was a relatively new infrastructure of early years services. Two changes were particularly damaging: ring-fence funding for early years services was removed and local authority budgets were drastically cut. The increased commitments on childcare meant there was even less funding available for children centres, so integrated local services for families have been disappearing at an alarming rate.[3] Policies designed to achieve two aims – improved child outcomes and female labour market participation – have become increasingly focused on the latter. The recent expansion of free childcare to 30 hours for working parents is a major investment in what has become a core service for most young children, but it is expensive, the major cost being staff. The low wages of childcare workers have resulted in two factors that affect quality: recruiting staff with good qualifications and retaining staff. The aims set out in 2004 to build a qualified workforce and improve management and leadership in early years settings became increasingly watered down.[4] It can be argued that from the start of the expansion of free hours, childcare staff qualification requirements were too low, which may explain in part the very slow progress in narrowing the gap in school readiness. The continued expansion of free childcare during the years of austerity was not matched by improved qualifications, or staff pay and conditions. Hence recruitment of highly qualified and experienced staff continues to be challenging. The pattern of spending on the early years over the last 20 years is revealing. Overall spending on the free entitlement and support for childcare costs through tax credits and the tax system has risen substantially since 2000, but in recent years it has become significantly more skewed to working parents as a whole rather than supporting low-income families.[5]

The fact that there have been some unequivocally good policies over this period does not mean that there are not things to learn. The first decade of the new millennium initiated what has become a new cornerstone of the welfare state with entitlements to free early years provision for every child in the UK. However, there remain differences in the take-up of early years places by socio-economic group, special educational needs, disability, ethnicity and region. There is mixed evidence on the impact of early years provision on children's educational outcomes, with the major Effective Pre-School, Primary and Secondary Education project (EPPSE) study showing lasting educational effects to GCSE, especially for disadvantaged children in quality settings, but other studies showing small impacts that fade over time.[6] Quantity of childcare has been prioritised over quality. The evidence for the impact of Sure Start has grown, but meanwhile the service has been drastically reduced. In retrospect, it was expanded too quickly; better to have had time to deliver it effectively in poor areas first.[7]

What next?

Ending child poverty has always required a two-pronged approach: employment and social security at suitable rates to lift families out of poverty, and family support services, including early education and care which is of sufficient quality to ensure children from less-advantaged homes experience quality care. Family income is critical, and so is family expenditure. We cannot end child poverty if basics like housing, transport, and childcare are unaffordable, and affordability is often locally determined. For early years services to improve, investment is needed to raise the training and qualifications of the workforce, to improve pay and conditions, as well as improving pedagogy and practice within early years settings. Reintroducing the Graduate Leader Fund as suggested by the Education Policy Institute would be an effective way to start.[8] A priority is to build on the wealth of learning from Sure Start programmes to reboot children's centres in deprived areas. A Sure Start integrated service package could be developed in other early years settings to meet the needs of children living in poverty, who are not living in deprived areas.

Given what is now known about infant development, maternity and paternity pay needs to be raised to living wage levels and paid leave extended to a full year. We need more incentives for fathers to take up their entitlements such as the 'take it or lose it' approaches that have been tried and tested in Scandinavia and Germany. So far, childcare for under-twos has largely been ignored. Subsidised childcare for under-twos needs to be expanded, including childminding. Offering one year of paid leave without improving both the quantity and quality of care for children aged from 12–24 months makes no sense. More efforts need to be made for innovative solutions that combine the quality inherent in group early education and the flexibility of home-based care. Having made significant progress in the early part of the 2000s, we have lost ground and weakened what was a strong start. We not only need to catch up, we need to significantly improve the offer for children, mothers and fathers.

In summary, much progress was made in the first decade of this century on support for families with young children, but new policies did not have enough time to become embedded in local areas. Progress has stalled and, on some issues, gone into reverse. The next decade needs significant investment that takes account of new work patterns for parents, as well as future skills demands within the workforce. Communication skills, teamwork, attention to task and self-regulation will all be needed in the future and are part of the core curriculum of good early years services. We can meet the aims of reducing poverty, enabling women to enter the workforce and improving child development, but only with significant new investment and learning from the past about what has and has not been effective.

Notes and references

1   Cattan and others, *The Health Effects of Sure Start*, Institute for Fiscal Studies, 2019

2   Brewer and others, *Free childcare and parents' labour supply: is more better?*, IFS Working Paper, Institute for Fiscal Studies, 2016, cited in N Eisenstadt and C Oppenheim, *Parents, Poverty and the State: 20 years of evolving family policy*, Policy Press, 2019

3   Smith and others, *Stop Start: survival, decline or closure? Children's centres in England*, Sutton Trust, 2018

4   S Bonetti, *Early Years Workforce Development in England: key ingredients and missed opportunities*, Education Policy Institute, 2020

5   J Britton, L Farquharson and L Sibieta, *2019 Annual Report on Education Spending in England*, Institute for Fiscal Studies, 2019

6   See N Eisenstadt and C Oppenheim, *Parents, Poverty and the State: 20 years of evolving family policy*, Policy Press, 2019, for fuller discussion of the evidence.

7   N Eisenstadt, *Providing a Sure Start: how government discovered early childhood*, Policy Press, 2011

8   S Bonetti, *Early Years Workforce Development in England: key ingredients and missed opportunities*, Education Policy Institute, 2020

Thirteen

Universalism: shifting the balance

Fran Bennett and Ruth Lister

Universal benefits[1] and services bind society together and can help maintain public support for social provision. Most developed welfare states have a mix of different kinds of benefits and services; but countries with all-encompassing and generous systems generally tend to have lower levels of poverty and better redistributive outcomes overall.[2] A recent study found that targeting benefits on children mattered even more for reducing child poverty than generally targeting those on lower incomes.[3] And globally, there is a 'growing appetite for universal approaches to direct support'.[4]

The arguments for universal services such as free healthcare for all are generally accepted in the UK. But there are also good arguments for universal provision of social security benefits, and other services for children. Here, we focus on child benefit, but also look more briefly at universalism in services, including childcare and free school meals.

In the UK benefits system generally, including support for children, there has been a long-term trend (with some exceptions and interruptions) towards the marginalisation of more universal benefits, as means testing has been extended in scope. We argue here for the reversal of this trend, and in favour of more emphasis on universalism.

In support of universalism

There are both principled and practical arguments in favour of universalism.

Universal benefits and services can help prevent poverty, rather than merely trying to relieve it after it has already struck. They promote social solidarity,[5] and redistribute resources without divisions into givers (taxpayers) and takers (recipients). This division has been shown to be largely a myth, in fact, with much of the welfare state redistributing across the life cycle, not just between people on different incomes.[6]

Universal benefits and services do not usually require someone to expose their resources (income and assets) to external scrutiny by officials in order to qualify. So they are better placed to uphold human dignity, which lies at the heart of a human rights perspective.[7] In addition, with families more fluid,[8] and the labour market often providing precarious employment with volatile incomes,[9] universal benefits and services can provide a grounding of genuine security.[10] And, for many in the UK claiming the new 'super means-tested benefit' universal credit, non-means-tested benefits give a safety net of regular income that can be relied on.

Practically, because take-up is higher, universal benefits and services often reach far more of those living in poverty than provisions targeted on them do.[11] They do not create a disincentive to someone trying to improve their income or assets, because they are usually not withdrawn as these increase.[12] Although they are likely to be more expensive in total because they reach more people, they tend to cost less to administer per recipient,[13] and involve fewer 'costs of compliance' for someone claiming.[14] Finally, and crucially, because more people have a stake in universal benefits and services, these are likely to attract wider and therefore more sustainable public support.[15]

Universal child benefit

There is currently a global push to urge countries to provide universal benefits for children.[16] In the UK, child benefit was introduced in the late 1970s, to replace child tax allowances as well as family allowances (the benefit for children introduced in the 1940s).[17] So among its multiple functions is horizontal redistribution – providing help with the costs of children, because those with children at any income level have less 'taxable capacity' (lower income compared with their needs) than those without.[18] And it redistributes resources over the life cycle, giving more when they are needed more.

Child benefit has many of the advantages of universal benefits and services described above. But in addition, it is an investment in the next generation by society, as children are '20 per cent of our population but 100 per cent of our future'.[19] And it demonstrates the value placed on children in their own right, as human beings, not just 'becomings' (future adults).[20]

Because child benefit is labelled as being for children, it is more likely to be spent on them.[21] It is paid to the mother or main carer, so gives her (usually) some degree of autonomy. This also means that it 'follows the child' through changes in family/partnership status[22] – particularly important in cases of domestic abuse, including financial coercion.[23]

Wages cannot – and should not – vary with family size. Child benefit supports lower-paid workers and those in 'in-work poverty' by being paid in as well as out of employment, without subsidising low pay (for which means-tested tax credits have sometimes been criticised).

Last but not least, these many functions of child benefit give it different constituencies of support and therefore arguably greater resilience to political pressures.

Policy since 2000

Labour governments (1997–2010) protected child benefit, while also emphasising means-tested provision, in particular tax credits, which they extended further up the income scale. They called this 'progressive universalism' (unfortunately in the process suggesting that universalism in itself is not progressive – which it can be, depending on how it is financed and the distribution of risks across the population). Social security, including child benefit, was also protected when the financial crisis hit in 2008.

But the Coalition (2010–15) and Conservative governments since then have reduced child benefit in real terms, meaning that it has now lost 23 per cent of its value.[24] In addition, tax credits and means-tested benefits for families have suffered a range of cuts, most benefits for those under pension age have been frozen for the past four years, and universal credit has cemented means testing at the heart of the social security system.

Not only that, but since 2013 parents (or their partners) who earn £50,000 per year or more must pay the 'high income child benefit tax charge',[25] which involves paying more tax, if one of them is receiving child benefit. By the time their income is £60,000 per year, this additional tax is equivalent to the value of the child benefit they or their partner receives. The only alternative is to give up child benefit.[26] In 2017/18, out of some 7.3 million recipients, over 800,000 (some 11 per cent) were paying the charge or giving up child benefit.[27] Unless thresholds are increased, a fifth of families will soon be losing some child benefit.[28]

This charge compromises both the universal nature of child benefit and the principles of independent taxation for men and women. It makes the tax system more complex and imposes high tax rates (even higher for those with several children) over a band of income. Someone who gives up their child benefit may miss out on pension rights later if they do not claim and then renounce it; and their children do not get a national insurance number automatically at age 16.

The government argument was that people on higher incomes should contribute to deficit reduction. But the high income child benefit tax charge only involved those claiming benefits – indeed, tax allowances were increased in real terms, meaning that together with the child benefit freeze the balance of the fiscal system was tilted against those with children. If it was thought that the better off should pay more tax, this should apply to all, not just those raising children now.

Where next?

In relation to **social security**, in view of the above arguments, we would argue that the balance between universal and means-tested benefits for children is now wrong, as is the balance between tax allowances for all income tax payers and child benefit for parents.

There should be a return to universal child benefit, by abolishing the high income child benefit tax charge. Child benefit should be uprated annually by at least inflation, and the value lost through freezing it in recent years restored. In the longer term, we must ensure a sustained commitment to child benefit by governments of whatever political persuasion.

Universal services for children are also important. Examples here include childcare, Sure Start/children's centres and universal extended schools provision, all of which were introduced and/or expanded by recent Labour governments. But more recently, while free early years education for three- and four-year-olds was expanded from 2017,[29] universalism has been compromised, by restricting the additional hours to parents in employment earning between a minimum and a maximum amount.[30] These restrictions should be abolished, and free early years education extended to all two- to four-year-olds.

Free school meals were taken in the opposite policy direction by the Coalition government, however, with the announcement in 2013 of universal provision for all children in reception classes and years one and two in primary school.[31] A recent CPAG report recommends extending free dinners to all school children, in part because the cafeteria system for older children can leave those on free school meals hungry and shamed.[32]

There is also growing support for free breakfasts in school, which are reported by teachers to help children from both an educational and health perspective.[33] These are usually provided on a universal basis, without a means test for children who receive them. However, this is different from Labour's universal extended schools provision, as schools are eligible for financial help from the government to pass on to the breakfast providers if at least half their children fall within certain disadvantaged categories[34] (with this funding now being extended beyond March 2020).

Conclusion

Universal services are important in part because they bring children from all backgrounds together, with benefits for all, but particularly for those from disadvantaged backgrounds.[35] Together with universal social security provision, this lays the foundation for a socially cohesive society from the start, in which everyone feels valued in their own right. Universalism should be one of the central principles of any future strategy to tackle child poverty in the UK from 2020 onwards.

Notes and references

1   'Universal' may be used in different ways. By 'universalism' what we mean here is not just comprehensive coverage of benefits and services, but also provision that is not means tested (paid only to those with low incomes and/or assets). It may not be available to every member of the population, but is usually for all in a specific category, such as children.

2   This was originally called the 'paradox of redistribution' (W Korpi and J Palme, 'The paradox of redistribution and strategies of equality: welfare state institutions, inequality and poverty, in the western countries', *American Sociological Review*, 63(5), 1998, pp661–89). It has been contested recently (eg, see L Kenworthy, *Progress for the Poor*, Oxford University Press, 2011), especially because of the 'deservingness' bestowed by means-tested help for those in work on low incomes. However, within countries McKnight (2015) has shown that periods of more targeted provision coincide with less reduction of inequality and poverty (taken from Box 3 in O Thévenon and others, *Child Poverty in the OECD: trends, determinants and policies to tackle it*, OECD, 2018, p48). See also D Gugushvili and T Laenen, *Twenty Years after Korpi and Palme's Paradox of Redistribution: what have we learned so far, and where should we take it from here?*, SPSW Working Paper No.5, Centre for Sociological Research, Catholic University of Leuven, 2019, especially p21.

3   E Barcena-Martin, MC Blanco-Arana and S Perez-Moreno, 'Social transfers and child poverty in European countries: pro-poor targeting or pro-child targeting?', *Journal of Social Policy*, 47(4), pp739–758 (although Jonathan Bradshaw argues that the level of benefits seems to be more important than their structure, in *Child poverty and child benefits in Europe*, briefing paper for Secure Futures, CPAG, 2020).

4   There is a Global Partnership for Universal Social Protection to Achieve the Sustainable Development Goals (agreed by many governments in 2015): www.social-protection.org/gimi/gess/NewYork.action?id=34.

5   J Gregory and T Horton, *The Solidarity Society*, Fabian Society, 2010

6   J Hills, *Good Times, Bad Times: the welfare myth of them and us*, Policy Press, 2014

7   EK Gubrium, S Pellissery and I Lodemel, *The Shame of It: global perspectives on anti-poverty policies*, Policy Press, 2013, in particular final chapter

8   F Bennett, 'The developed world', in *Megatrends and Social Security: family and gender*, International Social Security Association, 2017, pp10–26

9   A Haldane, Chief Economist, Bank of England, 'Climbing the job ladder', speech at Glanford Park Stadium, Scunthorpe, 23 July 2019

10 R Lister, *Seeking Security in an Increasingly Insecure World*, briefing paper for Secure Futures, CPAG, 2019

11 HM Revenue and Customs, *Child Benefit, Child Tax Credit and Working Tax Credit: take-up rates 2016 to 2017*, December 2018 (although the high income child benefit tax charge affects child benefit take-up)

12 R Farthing, *Save Child Benefit*, CPAG policy briefing, 2012

13 D Gugushvili, and D Hirsch, *Means Testing or Universalism: what strategies best address poverty?*, Centre for Research in Social Policy, Loughborough University, for Joseph Rowntree Foundation, 2014

14 F Bennett, M Brewer and J Shaw, *Understanding the Compliance Costs of Benefits and Tax Credits*, Institute for Fiscal Studies, 2009

15 As argued originally by W Korpi and J Palme, 'The paradox of redistribution and strategies of equality: welfare state institutions, inequality, and poverty in western countries', *American Sociological Review*, 63(5), 1998, pp661–687

16 A conference on 'Universal Child Grants' was organised by UNICEF, the International Labour Organization (ILO) and the Overseas Development Institute on 6–8 February 2019 in Geneva. See odi.org/events. See also unicef.org/social-policy/universal-child-grants; and L Yang and others, *Universal Child Benefit and Dignity and Shame*, UNICEF, 2019

17 F Bennett, with P Dornan, *Child Benefit: fit for the future*, CPAG policy briefing, CPAG, 2006

18 F Bennett, 'Taxation, couples and children', in J Bradshaw (ed), *Let's Talk About Tax*, CPAG, 2019, pp70–78

19 Gordon Brown MP, then Chancellor of the Exchequer, speech, reported in '"School gate mums" are new target', *The Guardian*, 15 April 2005

20 R Lister, 'Children (but not women) first: New Labour, child welfare and gender', *Critical Social Policy*, 26(2), 2006, pp315–335

21 SJ Lundberg, RA Pollak and TJ Wales, 'Do husbands and wives pool their resources? Evidence from the UK child benefit', *Journal of Human Resources*, 32(3), 1997, pp463–480

22 JC Brown, *Child Benefit: investing in the future*, CPAG, 1988

23 M Howard, *Benefits or Barriers? Making social security work for survivors of domestic violence and abuse across the UK's four nations*, Women's Budget Group, 2019

24 A Garnham, *Social Security: where have we been and where are we going?*, report for Secure Futures, CPAG, 2019

25 gov.uk/child-benefit-tax-charge; see also A Seely, *The High Income Child Benefit Charge (HICBC)*, Briefing Paper No.8631, House of Commons Library, 2019

26 For a discussion of the impact and issues, see F Bennett, 'Taxation, couples and children', in J Bradshaw (ed), *Let's Talk About Tax*, CPAG, 2019, pp70–78

27 Office of Tax Simplification, *Taxation and Life Events: simplifying tax for individuals*, 2019

28 C Emmerson, R Joyce and T Waters, 'Stealthy changes mean that soon one in five families with children will be losing some child benefit', *Observation*, Institute for Fiscal Studies, 2019

29 This expansion was from 15 to 30 hours per week in England. Provision varies in the devolved administrations. This applies to term time only. Providers have argued that insufficient funding is provided.

30 gov.uk/government/news/30-hours-free-childcare-launches

31 gov.uk/government/news/free-school-lunch-for-every-child-in-infant-school

32 R O'Connell, A Knight and J Brannen, *Living Hand to Mouth: children and food in low-income families*, CPAG (now open access), 2019

33 *Making the Case for School Breakfasts: improved educational and health outcomes for children*, Magic Breakfast, 2019

34 National School Breakfast Programme, *Food for Thought*, 2019

35 L Gambaro, K Stewart and J Waldfogel (eds), *An Equal Start? Providing quality early education and care for disadvantaged children*, Policy Press in association with University of Chicago Press, 2014

Fourteen

Schools and child poverty: from extended schools to closing the attainment gap. Where to from here?

Karen Laing and Liz Todd

The role of schools in relation to disadvantaged children has been subject to a dramatic shift in policy over the last two decades. For the first decade of the millennium, schools were increasingly expected to provide, be the location for, or signpost families to, support services and out-of-school activities. Since 2010, an increased focus on 'closing the gap' in attainment between children living in socio-economically deprived families and others has brought about a high-stakes school environment that can further disadvantage poor children. Developing inclusive education fit for the twenty-first century while maintaining high expectations for children involves developing asset-based approaches[1] embedded in high quality services and activities delivered from schools and in the curriculum they deliver.

During the early part of the century, policy in England asserted 'every child mattered'. Five broad, ambitious and imaginative outcomes were identified for children that applied to all services, including schools: to 'be healthy, stay safe, enjoy and achieve, make a positive contribution, and achieve economic well-being'.[2] From 1997 extended schools were trialled and then rolled out, giving every family access to childcare, parent support, out-of-hours' activities, and adult learning, delivered by schools in partnership with local providers.[3] Sure Start children's centres were central to extended services, offering local activities and services including co-located professionals such as speech therapists and family workers.

Our evaluation of full-service extended schools found evidence of cultural change in schools and some transformative impact on the attainment and wellbeing of individuals and families. These were due to the enthusiasm of practitioners in devising projects, schools establishing local strategic partnerships, short-term funding giving way to longer term capacity building, and a realignment of the accountability framework

(Ofsted valued community engagement). The benefits clearly outweighed the costs of working in this way. Improvements in educational achievement were expected to emerge over time. Margaret Hodge, then Minister of Children, Young People and Families, said in 2003 that it would take a minimum of 10 years for children's services to become fully joined up and effective in all they were trying to achieve. But this was not to be.

From 2010, a change in government heralded changes in policy advocating 'closing the gap' between children receiving means-based free school meals (a proxy for poverty), and others. In England, ring-fenced funding for extended services and children's centres was withdrawn along with the education maintenance allowance that supported young people in post-compulsory education. Schools were funded instead by 'pupil premium' (England), the 'pupil equity fund' (Scotland) and the 'pupil deprivation grant' (Wales) to provide educational support to the poorest children.

The broader educational context varies across the UK. In England, some schools have either chosen or were forced (via failed Ofsted inspections) to become 'academies', overseen directly by government instead of local authorities. Academisation was intended to raise educational standards but has resulted in a system that has become less equitable, with higher performing schools admitting fewer disadvantaged pupils, an increase in school exclusion, and some high-profile financial scandals and budget failures.[4] Scotland has continued to focus on a broad-based curriculum delivered by comprehensive, co-educational schools underpinned by the multi-agency approach, 'Getting it right for every child',[5] although policy to 'close the gap' was introduced through the National Improvement Framework. In Wales, schools fall behind the rest of the UK in socio-economic disparities in educational outcomes, despite a commitment to 'strong and inclusive schools committed to excellence, equality and well-being'.[6] In Northern Ireland, education is characterised by inequalities that intersect with religious divisions and socio-economic differences across the separate school systems. At the same time that the number of children living in poverty has increased, all UK jurisdictions have been subject to austerity. There have been cuts in services in some of the most economically disadvantaged areas and school budgets have fallen overall.

There is no evidence that 'closing the gap' is working. Recent research found that 'at the current rate of progress it would take a full 50 years to reach an equitable education system where disadvantaged pupils did not fall behind their peers during formal education to age 16'.[7]

The question of how schools can best respond to poverty remains. Actions to 'close the gap' have resulted in a high-stakes culture in which efforts to increase test scores have led to a narrower curriculum. Parents and children are not equally able to position themselves favourably with respect to assessment[8] and there is an increase in home tuition. Yet schools account for less than a third of the variance in children's school attainment. This can result in unfounded beliefs about undesirable family practices. In addition, schools can unwittingly create inequality. Widespread, yet hidden, stigmatisation can occur even where support for the most disadvantaged pupils is a stated priority.[9] Children from lower socio-economic groups are over-represented in lower sets[10] and our research suggested that behaviour is a common reason for this.[11] Some parents can see schools as hard to engage with.[12] We noted at the time a need for greater community involvement in extended schools,[13] echoed by CPAG's research.[14]

Poverty proofing is an assets-based audit process, developed by the charity Children North East and undertaken by independent researchers, that places children at the centre. All children in a school are consulted and a report is written on the measures that the school can take to remove stigmatisation and reduce the pressure of school costs on parents.[15] CPAG's Cost of the School Day Project (in partnership with Children North East) similarly helps school communities identify and overcome cost barriers that affect children's opportunities at school.[16]

Focusing on schooling alone is unlikely to lead to more equitable outcomes for children.[17] In particular, location matters. Children from disadvantaged families do far better in some places than others.[18] The inner cities are no longer the worst places to be, but remote rural, coastal and former industrial towns pose more problems for young people to get on. There is no correlation between affluence and social mobility – some of the most deprived areas have sustained high levels of social mobility, while some rich places such as West Berkshire deliver worse outcomes for disadvantaged children than Sunderland and Tower Hamlets. There are many reasons for this, but places where disadvantaged children do less well 'combine poor educational outcomes for young people from disadvantaged backgrounds with weak labour markets that have a greater share of low-skilled, low-paid employment than elsewhere in England, low proportions of managerial and professional jobs, and poor connectivity by transport, restricting opportunities still further'.[19] In London there has been a dramatic improvement in outcomes, due partly to a lack of many of these structural problems and partly to initiatives like the London Challenge.

We (a university) have been collaborating with schools, charities, cultural organisations, the local authority and an academy trust over the last five years to develop a children's community in a socio-economically deprived area of the North East. A 'children's community' brings together a range of existing services, local government, charities, cultural organisations and businesses in a specific geographical area to work in a co-ordinated way to tackle childhood disadvantage, with a specific focus, from cradle to career, on all the contexts in which children live and learn.[20] Organisations work together and with the community to evolve asset-based approaches to disadvantage. We started by working together to provide a more co-ordinated approach to primary-secondary transition and to summer activities for children, and are now developing a local play strategy and using a community organising approach to enable parents to achieve changes that they have identified. Our children's community draws on the best learning from extended schools, implemented in the current policy environment and in the context of austerity.

Leat's[21] project-based learning for the twenty-first century is an example of an asset – and community-based approach to the school curriculum, in which a school collaborates with other organisations and adopts processes of doing and thinking driven by curiosity. Young people develop skills to make sense of new information and experiences for themselves, and are encouraged to be critical and questioning, assuming as much responsibility as possible for their own learning. It often results in products such as videos, reports, presentations, performances, artworks or decisions of use to the community or partner organisation. For example, young people from a primary school worked on a Victorian history project with staff from Newcastle University's library archive and education and computing science departments, and results were displayed digitally.

Previous attempts at intervention, while well-meaning, have taken a 'deficit' approach by focusing on a community's problems, needs and deficiencies, and responding by providing services to fill the gaps and fix the problems. There is no golden bullet to address inequalities in educational attainment, but what we suggest is needed is a culture in which schools can enact an asset-based rather than a deficit-based approach to children and communities. This means accepting that children and families that are disadvantaged will have capacity, skills, knowledge, and connections within a community, and schools can play a role in enabling and valuing these assets. An asset-based approach does not replace investment in services or work to tackle the structural causes of inequality, but aims for a balance between community collaboration and service delivery.[22]

Notes and references

1 An asset-based approach focuses on people's strengths and resources and on community organisations, businesses and services available to a locality, as opposed to defining a community or locality solely in deficit terms.

2 Department for Education and Skills, *Every Child Matters*, Cm 5860, 2003, retrieved from A Dyson and others, 'From school to children's community: the development of Manchester Communication Academy, England, in HA Lawson and D Van Veen (eds), *Developing Community Schools, Community Learning Centers, Extended-service Schools and Multiservice Schools: international exemplars for practice, policy, and research*, Springer International, 2016 pp277–302; A Dyson, A Millward and L Todd, *A Study of 'Extended' Schools Demonstration Projects*, Research Report RR381, Department for Education and Skills, 2002

3 C Cummings, A Dyson and L Todd, *Evaluation of the Extended Schools Pathfinder Projects*, Research Report RR530, Department for Education and Skills, 2004; C Cummings, A Dyson and L Todd, *Beyond the School Gates: can full service and extended schools overcome disadvantage?*, Routlege, 2011; H Carpenter and others, *Extended Services Subsidy Pathfinder in Schools: evaluation*, Department for Education, Research Report RR042, 2010, retrieved from G Crozier and J Davies, 'Hard to reach parents or hard to reach schools? A discussion of home–school relations, with particular reference to Bangladeshi and Pakistani parents', *British Educational Research Journal*, 33(3), 2007, pp295–313; A Dyson, A Millward and L Todd, *A Study of 'Extended' Schools Demonstration Projects*, Research Report RR381, Department for Education and Skills, 2002

4 T Greany and R Higham, *Hierarchy, Markets and Networks: analysing the 'self-improving school-led system' agenda in England and the implications for schools*, UCL Institute of Education Press, 2018

5 Scottish Executive, *Getting It Rright for Every Child: proposals for action*, 2005

6 Welsh Government, *Education in Wales: our national mission. Action plan 2017–21*, 2017, retrieved from C Vincent and C Maxwell, 'Parenting priorities and pressures: furthering understanding of "concerted cultivation"', *Discourse: Studies in the Cultural Politics of Education*, 37(2), 2016, pp269–81

7 J Andrews, D Robinson and J Hutchinson, *Closing the Gap? Trends in educational attainment and disadvantage*, Education Policy Institute, 2017

8 SJ Ball, 'New class inequalities in education: why education policy may be looking in the wrong place! Education policy, civil society and social class', *International Journal of Sociology and Social Policy*, 30(3), 2010, pp155–166; C Vincent and C Maxwell, 'Parenting priorities and pressures: furthering understanding of "concerted cultivation"', *Discourse: Studies in the Cultural Politics of Education*, 37(2), 2016, pp269–81

9 L Mazzoli Smith and L Todd, 'Conceptualising poverty as a barrier to learning through "Poverty proofing the school day": the genesis and impacts of stigmatisation', *British Educational Research Journal*, 45(2), 2010, pp356–371

10 B Francis and others, 'Exploring the relative lack of impact of research on "ability grouping" in England: a discourse analytic account', *Cambridge Journal of Education*, 47(1), 2017, pp1–17

11 L Mazzoli Smith and L Todd, *Poverty Proofing the School Day: evaluation and development report*, Research Centre for Learning and Teaching, Newcastle University, 2016

12 G Crozier and J Davies, 'Hard to reach parents or hard to reach schools? A discussion of home–school relations, with particular reference to Bangladeshi and Pakistani parents', *British Educational Research Journal*, 33(3), 2007, pp295–313

13 C Cummings, A Dyson and L Todd, 'Towards extended schools? How education and other

professionals understand community-oriented schooling', *Children and Society*, 21, pp189–200

14 M Haddad, H Lambie-Mumford and L Sims, *Extended Schools*, CPAG, 2018

15 L Mazzoli Smith and L Todd, *Poverty Proofing the School Day: evaluation and development report*, Research Centre for Learning and Teaching, Newcastle University, 2016, retreived from L Mazzoli Smith and L Todd, 'Conceptualising poverty as a barrier to learning through "Poverty proofing the school day": the genesis and impacts of stigmatisation', *British Educational Research Journal,* 45(2), 2010, pp356–371

16 cpag.org.uk/cost-of-the-school-day

17 D Muijs, 'Effectiveness and disadvantage in education: can a focus on effectiveness aid equity in education?, in C Raffo and others, *Education and Poverty in Affluent Countries*, Routledge, 2009, Chapter 6

18 Social Mobility Commission, *State of the Nation 2017: social mobility in Great Britain*, November 2017

19 See note 18, page v

20 A Dyson and others, 'From school to children's community: the development of Manchester Communication Academy, England, in HA Lawson and D Van Veen (eds), *Developing Community Schools, Community Learning Centers, Extended-service Schools and Multi-service Schools: international exemplars for practice, policy, and research*, Springer International, 2016, pp277–302

21 D Leat, *Enquiry and Project Based Learning: students, school and society*, Routledge, 2017

22 J Foot and T Hopkins, *A Glass Half-full: how an asset approach can improve community health and well-being*, Improvement and Development Agency, 2010

Fifteen

Children's health from the front line: poverty is the main driver of inequalities in health in the UK

David Taylor-Robinson and Davara Bennett

There are large and persistent health inequalities in the UK and, at the moment, they are getting worse. We know that these inequalities have their origins in childhood, and that child poverty is a major driver of poor child health. The reality is stark. A child born in the most disadvantaged tenth of areas of the UK can expect to live around 10 years fewer than a child born in the most advantaged tenth of areas.[1] The gap increases to almost 20 years when we consider years lived in good health, so-called healthy life expectancy.[2] This reality is shameful because it is by no means inevitable. Health inequalities are widely considered preventable.

At first

In 1999, Tony Blair pledged to end child poverty by 2020. This was one element of New Labour's broader inequality strategy which included the English Health Inequalities Strategy, regarded as the world's largest experiment in tackling health inequalities. Recognising the importance of the childhood period in generating health inequalities, these strategies included a key focus on improving the living conditions of families with children.

The inequality strategy spanned a raft of interlinked policies and interventions to address the root causes of poor health – poverty and poor standards of living. There were increased levels of spending, according to local need, on a range of social programmes to support families, on preventative public health programmes, and on improving healthcare access.[3] Some actions were targeted to poor areas – for example, regeneration efforts and the initial roll-out of Sure Start children's centres providing early years childcare and education. Others were universal. Child poverty was addressed through action on the tax and benefit system, and the introduction of the national minimum wage. There were also interventions to improve education, housing, and employment which helped to support, in particular, struggling families with children.[4]

Two decades on, new research is beginning to shed light on the impressive impacts of the co-ordinated effort to address health inequalities in England.[5] Although the health inequalities strategy failed to hit its stated targets, the outcomes of complex interventions often emerge in time. It is now clear that inequalities in life expectancy and child mortality between rich and poor areas narrowed. Inequalities in mortality amenable to health care decreased during the strategy period. There were also reductions in inequalities for key determinants of child health: unemployment, child poverty, housing quality, educational attainment.[6] These initial impacts subsequently translated into benefits for health.

But then

Hard-won gains can quickly be lost.[7] The recession and the UK government's austerity programme brought this progress on health inequalities to an abrupt end.[8] Action on poverty stalled, and at the same time severe cuts to funding for local government services essential for child health hit the poorest places hardest.[9] As a consequence, funding for preventative children's services plummeted (Figure 15.1), with over a thousand children's centres closing since 2010. Local government funding has an important effect on health and, given the wealth of evidence indicating that greater investment in the early years of life reduces health inequalities,[10] the current disinvestment is of great concern.

In 2016, the child poverty targets were scrapped. The Welfare Reform and Work Bill removed the government's duty to end child poverty by 2020. Replacement targets were based on measures such as unemployment, family breakdown and parental behaviours, conflating the causes and consequences of poverty. There were many dissenting voices[12] and, as a result, one minor success was the retention of the income-based child poverty targets, revived in an amendment to the original bill after a showdown in the House of Lords.[13]

Child poverty is now rising dramatically. In 2014, there were 3.7 million children in England living in relative poverty after housing costs.[14] By 2017, this number had risen to 4.1 million, amounting to over 30 per cent

Figure 15.1:

Sure Start funding per child by quintile of local area income deprivation

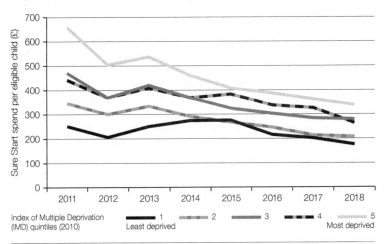

Index of Multiple Deprivation (IMD) quintiles (2010)

Least deprived ■■■■ 1　■ ■ ■ 2　■■■■ 3　■ ■ ■ 4　■ ■ ■ 5　Most deprived

Source: Data from Place-based Longitudinal Data Resource (PLDR)[11]

of all children in England. Independent predictions suggest a further six percentage point rise over the next five years, which will push child poverty to its highest level on record. By 2023/24, the proportion of children living in relative poverty is on course to hit 37 per cent, affecting an additional 1.1 million children.[15]

Numerous studies have shown that child poverty is toxic for child health.[16] We recently looked at data from the UK Millennium Cohort Study, a nationally representative sample of thousands of children born in 2000.[17] Over half the children were in poverty at some point up to the age of 14, and one-fifth of the children had always lived in poverty. All other things held equal, persistent poverty tripled children's likelihood of having mental health problems in adolescence, and doubled the likelihood of being obese or having a chronic illness.

So, predictably, we have witnessed a great leap backwards for child health in the UK.[18] After a period of improvement, inequalities in life expectancy at birth and child mortality are widening once more. Inequalities in the modern epidemics of childhood – mental health problems and obesity – are rising.[19] Infant mortality is on the rise, and it is rising most in poor areas.[20] This represents a marked reversal of fortunes since the English Health Inequalities Strategy (2000–2010), which was associated with decreases in inequalities in infant mortality and life expectancy in England.[21] Improvements in life expectancy at birth have stalled, and life expectancy is now going backwards, especially for women living in disadvantaged areas.[22] These demographic changes are highly unusual, and deeply concerning: infant mortality and life expectancy at birth are sensitive indicators of the overall health of societies, and act as an early warning system for future adverse trends. The rate of children entering local authority care is also rising, and the vast inequalities between rich and poor areas are increasing relative to previous trends.[23] There is evidence suggesting that child poverty is a key determinant of the risk of children experiencing neglect or abuse and subsequently entering care.[24] These children are among the most vulnerable in our society, and we, as a society, are responsible for their health and wellbeing. Offering early support to struggling families can prevent issues from escalating, and help keep children safe, but these preventative services have been cut most in the areas of greatest need.

What now?

To tackle the growing crisis, we need action on three fronts. Firstly, the government must back a social security system that ensures an adequate quality of life for all families with children. This must begin with the provision of sufficient income support.[25] It is clearly within our power to protect vulnerable members of society against poverty, as with the 'triple lock' that stabilised incomes for the elderly. Secondly, in order to mitigate the consequences of poverty, we need a fresh commitment to universal services and a focus on proportionate universalism (services for everyone, but with a scale and intensity that is proportionate to the level of need) with a shift in investment towards the early years wherever possible. At the moment, as Figure 15.1 illustrates, we are seeing the opposite. Thirdly, we need to measure and understand the problem of poverty, and assess the impact of action. For example, our recent analysis of the roll-out of universal credit shows large negative effects on mental health for adults – but the impact on children is not yet clear.[26] Assessing the health inequalities impacts of policies is key to designing better policy in the future.

As a child public health doctor working in a disadvantaged city, on the front line, the impacts of poverty on children's health and life chances are obvious. My paediatric colleagues deal with the consequences of poverty in emergency departments and hospital wards on a daily basis –

from unnecessary child deaths to poorly controlled chronic conditions such as asthma and diabetes. My colleagues in the city council deal with the social fall-out – from children turning up to school hungry unable to learn, to the unsustainable pressure on services due to the rising numbers of children in need. The data show that far from the UK entering a new 'golden age',[27] we now seem to be aspiring to levels of poverty, inequality and poor child health seen in the USA, which has the worst record of any rich country. As the United Nations has recently highlighted, rising poverty in the UK is the outcome of a set of policy decisions.[28] Political choice has jeopardised the health and life chances of a generation of children in the UK; political choice is now needed to reverse the situation. It is time for the government to safeguard children by building and sustaining a social security system that protects children from poverty.

Notes and references

1   M Whitehead, N McInroy and C Bambra, *Due North: report of the Inquiry on Health Equity for the North*, University of Liverpool and the Centre for Economic Strategies, 2014

2   Office for National Statistics, 'Comparing inequalities in life expectancy between 2012 to 2014 and 2015 to 2017, England', *Health State Life Expectancies by National Deprivation Deciles, England and Wales: 2015 to 2017*, March 2019

3   C Law, C Parkin and H Lewis, 'Policies to tackle inequalities in child health: why haven't they worked (better)?', *Archives of Disease in Childhood*, 97, 2012, pp301–303

4   B Barr, J Higgerson and M Whitehead, 'Investigating the impact of the English health inequalities strategy: time trend analysis', *BMJ*, 358, 2017

5   B Barr, J Higgerson and M Whitehead, 'Investigating the impact of the English health inequalities strategy: time trend analysis', *BMJ*, 358, 2017; and T Robinson and others, 'The impact of New Labour's English health inequalities strategy on geographical inequalities in infant mortality: a time-trend analysis', *Journal of Epidemiology and Community Health*, 73(6), 2019, pp564–8

6   B Barr, J Higgerson and M Whitehead, 'Investigating the impact of the English health inequalities strategy: time trend analysis', *BMJ*, 358, 2017

7   D Taylor-Robinson, M Whitehead and B Barr, 'Great leap backwards', *BMJ*, 349, 2014

8   B Barr and D Taylor-Robinson, 'Recessions are harmful to health', *BMJ*, 354, 2016

9   D Taylor-Robinson, 'Austerity measures hit the sickest hardest', *BMJ*, 347, 2020

10 D Taylor-Robinson, B Barr and M Whitehead, 'Stalling life expectancy and rising inequalities in England', *The Lancet*, 394(10216), 2019, pp2238–9

11 Place-based Longitudinal Data Resource, available at https://pldr.org

12 All Party Parliamentary Group on Health in All Policies, *Inquiry: Child Poverty and Health : the impact of the Welfare Reform and Work Bill 2015–16*, 2016

13 'Bill documents – Welfare Reform and Work Act 2016', UK Parliament, available at https://services.parliament.uk/bills/2015-16/welfarereformandwork/documents.html

14 Department for Work and Pensions, *Households Below Average Income* (HBAI) statistics, available at gov.uk/government/collections/households-below-average-income-hbai--2

15 A Corlett, *The Living Standards Outlook 2019*, Resolution Foundation, 2019

16 K Cooper and K Stewart, 'Does money affect children's outcomes? An update', http://sticerd.

lse.ac.uk/case/_new/research/money_matters/report.asp

17 ETC Lai and others, 'Poverty dynamics and health in late childhood in the UK: evidence from the Millennium Cohort Study', *Archives of Disease in Childhood*, 104(11), 2019, pp1049–55

18 D Taylor-Robinson, M Whitehead and B Barr, 'Great leap backwards', *BMJ*, 349, 2014; and R Viner and others, *Child Health in England in 2030: comparisons with other wealthy countries*, Royal College of Paediatrics and Child Health, 2018

19 S Davies, *Time to Solve Childhood Obesity: an independent report by the Chief Medical Officer*, Department of Health and Social Care, 2019; and VS Straatmann and others, 'How do early-life factors explain social inequalities in adolescent mental health? Findings from the UK Millennium Cohort Study', *Journal of Epidemiology and Community Health*, 73(11), 2019, pp1049–60; and S Collishaw and others, 'Brief report: a comparison of child mental health inequalities in three UK population cohorts', *European Child and Adolescent Psychiatry*, 28(11), 2019, pp1547–9

20 'Assessing the impact of rising child poverty on the unprecedented rise in infant mortality in England, 2000–2017: time trend analysis', *BMJ Open*, https://bmjopen.bmj.com/content/9/10/e029424

21 B Barr, J Higgerson and M Whitehead, 'Investigating the impact of the English health inequalities strategy: time trend analysis', *BMJ*, 358, 2017; and T Robinson and others, 'The impact of New Labour's English health inequalities strategy on geographical inequalities in infant mortality: a time-trend analysis', *Journal of Epidemiology and Community Health*, 73(6), 2019, pp564–8

22 D Taylor-Robinson, B Barr and M Whitehead, 'Stalling life expectancy and rising inequalities in England', *The Lancet*, 394(10216), 2019, pp2238–9

23 E Lai, D Taylor-Robinson and D Bennett, 'RF26 Quantifying inequalities in looked after children in England', *Journal of Epidemiology and Community Health*, 73, 2019, A66–A67

24 P Bywaters and others, *The Relationship Between Poverty, Child Abuse and Neglect: an evidence review*, Joseph Rowntree Foundation, 2016

25 T Robinson and others, 'The impact of New Labour's English health inequalities strategy on geographical inequalities in infant mortality: a time-trend analysis', *Journal of Epidemiology and Community Health*, 73(6), 2019, pp564–8

26 S Wickham and others. 'Effects on mental health of a UK welfare reform, universal credit: a longitudinal controlled study', *Lancet Public Health*, 5(3), 2020, ppE157–E164

27 'The *Observer* view on the Queen's speech and Boris Johnson's promises', *Observer* editorial, 22 December 2019, theguardian.com

28 'Poverty is a political choice', *The Lancet Public Health*, 3(12), 2018

Sixteen

Fixing the housing crisis: the importance of place and where poverty is lived

Polly Neate

Without ending the national emergency that our housing crisis has become, there will never be an end to child poverty. It is that simple. I am talking about the toddler I met in a tiny hostel room that still swallowed all his mother's benefits, with wall-to-wall beds, nowhere to play, and a dirty and intimidating corridor leading to a tiny shared bathroom and kitchen.

Yet successive governments have seemingly settled into a cosy sort of helplessness, offering very little intervention, and destroying what little support exists for those worst affected. The 1999 pledge to end child poverty spoke of incomes before and after housing costs as a factor; however, there were very few references to housing as part of the solutions. Without investing in social housing, child poverty will not end.

Those at the sharpest end of our housing emergency are children: the 127,000 children who are now homeless and living in temporary accommodation (TA) in England. Local authorities are obliged to provide temporary accommodation for families that are homeless, although many over-use the 'intentionally homeless' get-out if they think they won't be challenged. Families can be trapped for years in this unstable, often over-crowded and unsuitable accommodation because of the chronic shortage of social housing. The number of homeless children living in temporary accommodation in England was first recorded in 2004. In that year 121,590 homeless children were living in temporary accommodation. This reduced to 68,770 in 2011. Since then, the number of homeless children living in temporary accommodation has been increasing and there are now over 127,000 homeless children in England.

From the mid-2000s, the government encouraged housing author-ities to prevent statutory homelessness 'by using private renting' rather than temporary accommodation. There was also a concerted effort between 2001 and 2010 to reduce the number of homeless households placed in bed and breakfast (B&B) accommodation, particularly those with children.[1]

Figure 16.1:

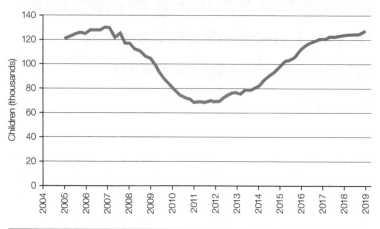

Homeless children in temporary accommodation in England

Source: Ministry of Housing, Communities and Local Government, *Statutory homelessness live tables*, Table TA1

Since 2010, there has been a number of welfare cuts and reforms, including cuts to housing benefit, or Local Housing Allowance (LHA), and the introduction of the benefit cap, that have all contributed to a rise in temporary accommodation.

The impact of homelessness, insecure housing and severely poor housing conditions on children cannot be overstated. A report by Shelter in 2006[2] found that poor housing conditions can lead to a 25 per cent higher risk of severe ill health and disability during childhood and early adulthood: meningitis, asthma and slow growth, a greater chance of mental health and behavioural problems, lower educational attainment, and a greater likelihood of unemployment and poverty in the future.

More recently, we interviewed GPs across the country in 2017 about their experiences with patients experiencing poor housing and homelessness.[3] We found a deep concern among doctors about the impact of insecurity of housing and the conditions children were living in. One doctor said: '...obviously, there are respiratory conditions, for example. You know, your house is wet and mouldy, that kind of thing, that can have an effect on conditions like asthma.' Another said: 'In the children, they just tend to get a little bit, sometimes withdrawn, sometimes a bit anxious and angry.'

A similar study of teachers in 2017 found homeless children were struggling to concentrate in class, make friends, achieve their potential.[4]

So why are there so many families who cannot afford anywhere decent to live in the UK?

The answer is frustratingly obvious and simple: nowhere near enough homes are being built that people on low incomes can rent. Forty years of inaction by consecutive governments have seen a catastrophic decline in social housing. The chronic lack of social homes leaves no choice but the private sector. And for families on a low income, getting by in the private sector is near impossible.

Governments have been intimidated by NIMBYism and the billions to be made out of disregarding true affordability in the housing market, while a shift in our national culture has stigmatised people living on housing estates or receiving benefits. At the same time, governments have removed the protection that existed to ensure that poverty did not mean homelessness.

The freeze on housing benefit for those renting privately – Local Housing Allowance (LHA) – in 2016 means that now, in 97 per cent of areas in England, it does not cover the cheapest third of rents. In a third of the country, it does not even cover the bottom 10 per cent of local rents. Shelter's recent research showed that for those on the lowest incomes, the average shortfall is more than £113 a month. And our private renters' survey,[5] and the daily experience of staff providing our face-to-face services, show the impossible choices families face, and the impact these have on their children.

Of those renting privately and claiming LHA, 36 per cent have had to cut back on food, and nearly one in five people have had to cut back on children's clothes, toys and school uniforms. Other families must squeeze into properties that are too small in order to afford the rent: the overcrowding rate amongst LHA claimants is almost twice that of other private renters. Families also frequently settle for properties that are damp, structurally unsound or in need of multiple repairs: a third of private renters receiving LHA live in non-decent accommodation, according to the English Housing Survey 2016/17.

Poor housing and homelessness are now inevitable, because while profits, capital gains and long-term security continue to be found in property for some, nothing has been done to secure the right to a safe home for all.

That can change. For a start, it is urgent to reinstate some protection for people who cannot afford both to rent and to feed and clothe their children. That means returning LHA to a level at which it covers the cheapest third of local rented homes. Doing that would immediately lift thousands of children out of poverty.

But in the longer term, there is only one way to end the current situation that is turning the lives of children we at Shelter see every day into an unwinnable struggle against the odds. That is to build social housing. At least 90,000 social homes a year for 20 years. The government needs to rediscover its ambition and stop hiding behind developers and NIMBYs. It does not have to be difficult or frightening. It is not going to kill the spirit of self-sufficiency or turn lovely areas into 'grim estates'. The opposite in fact. A safe home is where opportunity grows. Any efforts to end child poverty will fail without investing in social housing.

Very recently, one of our front line workers told me about a 12-year-old girl who had lived all her life in temporary and emergency accommodation: B&Bs and hostels, often in a single room with her mum and little brother. Seven different buildings, which cannot be called homes. She had never invited a school friend round, not once. For her, and the thousands like her, the government must invest in building more social housing, and do it now.

Notes and references

1   W Wilson and C Barton, *Households in Temporary Accommodation (England)*, Briefing Paper No.02110, House of Commons Library, February 2020

2   L Harker, *Chance of a Lifetime: the impact of bad housing on children's lives*, Shelter, 2006

3   Shelter and ComRes, *The Impact of Housing Problems on Mental Health*, Shelter, 2017

4   A Digby and E Fu, *Impacts of Homelessness on Children – research with teachers*, Shelter and Kantar Public, 2017

5   Survey results are from an online YouGov/Shelter survey of 3,995 private renters in England, Aug–Sept 2019, weighted according to official statistics.

Seventeen

Let's talk about tax[1]

Alan Buckle

The road untaken

The fight against child poverty must be funded and therefore good tax policies are essential. So it is not surprising that the story of child poverty and tax in the last 20 years breaks down more or less into two halves, dominated by two quite different chancellors.

In the years following Tony Blair's Toynbee Hall speech in 1999, Gordon Brown was already showing himself to be a bold chancellor with regard to tax. He levied a windfall tax on utilities and raised substantial revenues by shaking up tax relief for mortgage payments, and raised more revenue by changing the way pension funds were taxed. The main beneficiary of this extra tax was tax credits,[2] the new approach to social security payments which helped many families with children out of poverty.

George Osborne was just as bold in his austerity programme to pay down debt. But his choice was very different. He paid down debt largely by cutting spending rather than raising taxes. The spending cuts focused on social security. While some taxes were increased – principally VAT, from 17.5 per cent to 20 per cent, which hit the poorest hardest – other tax rates were cut, starting with corporation tax. The seeds of rising child poverty were sown.

Since 2010, the bottom 10 per cent by income have lost 11 per cent of their income – by far the most of any group. And within this bottom 10 per cent, families with children lost even more – 20 per cent of household income. Among the top half of earners, all but the highest earning 10 per cent have gained through 'reforms' and even the very highest earners have begun to benefit since 2015.[3]

A well-funded social security system is affordable – through an effective and progressive tax system. But for the moment, we have chosen the opposite. There is an interesting precedent from the years after World War Two. Tax rates rose sharply – income tax peaked at 83 per cent, (unearned income was taxed at 98 per cent). This was driven by financial need and a sense of fairness, but also a feeling that the whole population had shouldered the burden of the war whereas capital had not. Since the financial crisis, the poorest families have suffered the most, while capital in the form of the banks, was rescued by the government. There is a need for a new balance of contribution to be struck.

Tax is the answer: rates, reliefs, responsibility

The package of changes to universal credit recommended by CPAG to kick start an end to child poverty would cost £20.8 billion.[4] There is not space in this chapter to set out the whole tax reform agenda but here are a few examples of how to cover that £20.8 billion needed and relaunch the fight against child poverty.

Tax rates

There has been a drive since 2010 to position the UK at the bottom end of corporation tax rates worldwide. Rates have fallen from 28 per cent to 19 per cent. While this might make sense for small countries which build their economies around tax – Singapore, Ireland and a host of tax havens – it makes no sense for a major western economy. Businesses make long-term reasoned investment decisions which require long-term, stable, credible taxes.

HMRC's own evaluation is that a 1 per cent increase in corporation tax would yield more than £2 billion a year.[5] The UK's rate of 19 per cent is now more than 10 per cent behind Germany and France, which have rates around 30 per cent.[6] It is possible to envisage an increase of around 10 percentage points, each worth £2 billion. This would fund most of the £20.8 billion package sought by CPAG for families with children.[7]

It is a similar story with rates of capital gains tax. Until 2008, capital gains from selling assets were taxed at the same rate as income tax rates. They are now taxed at far lower rates. It has been estimated[8] that raising capital gains tax rates so that capital gains are taxed at the same rates as earned income would yield up to £10 billion. Changes in behaviour would reduce this, but a large dent could be made in child poverty, nonetheless.

Tax reliefs

Our tax system is undermined by more than 1,000 tax reliefs and allowances which dramatically reduce revenues. Policy makers often invent tax allowances to gain quick publicity, but rarely do they test out other options or provide evidence that the tax allowance will achieve the desired behaviour before launch. Neither do they test whether it is value for money once it is up and running.

The most striking example is the tax deduction for pension contributions. The argument in its favour is that it encourages people to make themselves financially secure in retirement. However, most of the pension tax allowances have gone to provide future financial security to the highest paid people[9] who are likely to be financially secure in any case. At the same time, we deny financial security to families with children who need it now. The cost in 2018[10] was £37.2 billion of tax and £16.5 billion of national insurance. £53.7 billion in total. Restricting allowable pension pots far further could fund a large reduction in child poverty.

There are many more examples of ways to reform tax allowances. The Entrepreneurs Relief, which costs more than £2.4 billion a year, is widely viewed as irrelevant to investment decisions and therefore is wasted money.[11] ISAs and other investment incentives – which go largely to the better off – cost more than £6 billion each year.[12]

Responsibility for tax revenues

There is a need for greater accountability and responsibility in our tax regime. HMRC's assessment of the tax gap lost to error, avoidance and illegal activities is more than £35 billion.[13] The amount as a percentage of the total tax was 5.6 per cent in 2018 and has been more or less static in recent years. One cannot help but ask why a £35 billion gap remains so stubborn.

The National Audit Office's last full review of tax reliefs in 2014[14] was damning, and nothing much has changed since then. The National Audit Office found that HMRC does not collect data that would allow it to conclude on the effectiveness of tax reliefs and it found little evidence that HMRC evaluates tax reliefs to see if their objectives are being met. Yet we spend huge amounts in providing these reliefs.

The tax system does not work for many families

Even if the switch was flicked on tax changes to restart the fight against child poverty, wider reforms would be needed to ensure that the tax system works for those in most need. It is no good just to raise money – it needs to be raised from the right people in the right way.

Viewed through the lens of poverty in families with children, the system is fundamentally unfair. The poorest 10 per cent of families with children pay a higher percentage of their income in direct and indirect tax than any income groups. The other 90 per cent, pay similar percentages to each other.[15]

The wide variety of tax allowances for different kinds of income (earnings, capital gains, interest, dividends) means that those with a variety of unearned and earned income can receive £29,000[16] before tax is paid, far above the personal allowance of £12,500 which is available to normal workers.

Women, who often head the poorest families, have fared badly. Tax cuts since 2010 have been skewed to men[17] and the huge tax reliefs for pension contributions are claimed disproportionately by men.[18]

The old have advantages over the young, and therefore over young families. Those over retirement age no longer pay national insurance on their earnings. Increasingly, repayments of student debt will come into play. And, of course, older people are more likely to benefit from lower taxes on unearned income, as they have most of the savings.

Is there hope for reform?

Imagine this. The Chancellor of the Exchequer announces a fundamental reform of the tax system. Tax rates that have fallen too low are restored, taxes are combined so that profits, earnings, capital gains and gifts are taxed in the same way. The system is simplified to remove most of the tax allowances and reliefs. All queries, returns and payments are made online. Far harsher penalties are introduced for those who try to avoid tax. Tax advisors are strictly regulated and as a result far fewer in number. We might even plan for a revival of national insurance, to cover the basics of the welfare state: the NHS, social care and social security.

Impossible? But such a reform programme is no more radical than the reform of social security through universal credit. This is now forecast to be completed in 2022, 12 years after its announcement, has caused huge suffering, yet has been stubbornly pursued. So, it is possible to envisage a more competent and humane reform of the tax system.

Advice to a reforming chancellor

It is a brave chancellor who would reform the tax system. Remember the poll tax which did for Margaret Thatcher, the Omnishambles budget that might have done for George Osborne or the end of the 10 per cent tax rate which shook even Gordon Brown.

Chancellors can be hamstrung from the start. Most Labour manifestos say little about tax reform and then chancellors have to make reforms piecemeal. Most Conservative manifestos say lots about tax but only about cutting it and therefore Conservative governments find reform impossible.

A recent Institute for Government report drew on the experiences of recent chancellors, advisors and civil servants to set out good advice for tax-reforming chancellors:[19] have a narrative and a road map, go early – make changes in your first budget, go large – one or two bold moves rather than lots of tinkering, and work from an evidence base rather than on a whim. Perhaps the role of the chancellor is too much for one person, and we need a second heavyweight alongside the chancellor who focuses solely on raising revenue.

What we do know is that there is great scope to raise the revenue needed to end child poverty – this chapter has given some examples. We know we have done this in the past. We can see from the years that followed the Toynbee Hall speech, that change is possible. We could again choose to take the road to the end of child poverty. That road is called 'tax'.

Notes and references

1   This chapter shares takes its title from a book edited by Professor Jonathan Bradshaw and published by CPAG. It partly draws on material and ideas from that book.
2   J Browne and D Phillips, *Tax and Benefit Reforms Under Labour*, IFS Briefing Note BN88, Institute for Fiscal Studies, 2010
3   P Bourquin, A Norris Keiller and T Waters, *The Distributional Impact of Personal Tax and Benefit Reforms, 2010 to 2019*, IFS Briefing Note BN270, Institute for Fiscal Studies, 2019. This paper also points out that at all income levels families of working age with children have lost out.

4   J Tucker, *Universal Credit: what needs to change to reduce child poverty and make it fit for families?*, CPAG, 2019

5   HM Revenue and Customs, *Direct Effects of Illustrative Tax Changes*, April 2019

6   KPMG, *Corporate Tax Rates Tables*, 2019

7   This is supported by an Institute for Fiscal Studies Observation from May 2017: H Miller, *Labour's Reversal of Corporate Tax Cuts Would Raise Substantial Sums But Comes With Important Trade-offs*. It suggests that an increase to 26 per cent would raise £19 billion a year in the medium term. It raises a concern that in the longer term, international investors might be deterred but recognises that at 26 per cent the UK rate would still be among the lowest corporate tax rates internationally.

8   S Nanda and H Parkes, *Just Tax: reforming the taxation of income from wealth and work*, Institute for Public Policy Research, 2019. This report models a number of changes to capital gains tax.

9   The total of pensions wealth is a good proxy for the claiming of tax allowances. This is reported by the Office for Budget Responsibility in its fiscal sustainability analytical paper: S Johal, P Mathews and D Taylor, *Private Pensions and Savings: the long-term effect of recent policy measures*, October 2016, based on Office for National Statistics, *Wealth and Asset Survey*, 2015.

10   HM Revenue and Customs, *Cost of Pension Tax Reliefs*, 2019

11   HM Revenue and Customs, *Estimated Costs of Principle Tax Reliefs*, 2019

12   HM Revenue and Customs, *Estimated Costs of Principle Tax Reliefs*, 2019

13   HM Revenue and Customs, *Measuring Tax Gaps*, 2019

14   National Audit Office, *The Effective Management of Tax Reliefs*, HC 785, 2014. A follow-up report in February 2020 noted that some improvements were being made but that these were 'very much in development' and would be insufficient.

15   Office for National Statistics, *Effects of Taxes and Benefits on Household Income: historical household-level data sets*, June 2018

16   See A Summers, 'Taxes on investment income and gains', in J Bradshaw (ed), *Let's Talk About Tax: how the tax system works and how to change it,* CPAG, 2019

17   Women's Budget Group, *Tax and Gender*, 2019

18   Women's Budget Group, *Pensions and Gender Inequality*, 2019

19   G Tetlow and others, *How to Be a Tax-Reforming Chancellor*, Institute for Government, December 2019 (updated in February 2020)

Eighteen

Secure futures for children and families: reforming social security

Sophie Howes

Introduction

Any government that is serious about ending child poverty for good cannot afford to ignore social security. We only have to look at the deep cuts to the social security budget over the last decade and the rising child poverty rates, to see that investing in the social security system is an essential first step. But as well as adequate investment, we also need to ask: what should the social security system look like?

Since our modern welfare state was created, the dominant trend in the development of our social security system has been ever more means testing. Sixty per cent of working-age benefit spending is now means tested, with other types of benefits playing a declining role.[1] Means testing itself has become more intensive in terms of frequency and the administrative burden placed on claimants, reaching a peak in universal credit. The main universal element of our system, child benefit, is worth less than ever and for higher earners it is clawed back in tax. The soaring cost of housing has meant large numbers of people are relying on means-tested help with housing costs, despite being in work. And contributory benefits, which provide support for people facing ill health or redundancy on the basis of national insurance contributions, have been eroded at such a scale that many people do not realise they exist and therefore may not make a claim even when they are entitled – except for retirement pension.

Taking a closer look at the last 20 years, under the Labour administration we saw a period of high investment in children's benefits, and the introduction of tax credits to provide light-touch means-tested support for families with children on a low income, both in and out of work, as part of the pledge to end child poverty. Tax credits were structured so that small amounts were payable to families relatively high up the earnings scale, under the so-called 'progressive universalist' agenda, and designed to feel like part of the tax system, not like 'benefits'. At the same time however, conditionality was intensified for the unemployed and lone parents, albeit backed by a new minimum wage, investment in childcare and high-quality employment support.

From 2010 onwards, we have seen heavy cuts to working-age benefits, and a move to replace most working-age benefits and tax credits with the single universal credit system, which has much more in common with out-of-work benefits than with tax credits. The creep of increasing conditionality has also continued, with more and more groups now subject to work-related requirements.

It is against this backdrop that CPAG has been considering what changes might be needed to our social security system, as part of our project 'Secure Futures for Children and Families'. To do this, we have gone back to the beginning and asked ourselves: what are the basic principles that should underpin the design and delivery of the social security system?

At CPAG we believe the social security system should:

• **Prevent and reduce poverty**.

• **Provide genuine income security** to children and families, whatever their circumstances.

• **Promote social solidarity** through the delivery of a system that is inclusive, respectful, and non-stigmatising.

The project also sets out principles for the design of the system. It should be simple to use and flexible enough to respond to individual needs, and ought to promote individual autonomy, empowering people to make choices that fit with their circumstances and give people control over their income. Mechanisms are needed to ensure that the voices of those who use, and work in, the system are heard, and that take-up is maximised with support for vulnerable claimants and a right to independent advice and representation. And finally, the system must be rights based, with claimant entitlements based on the law and with clear rights to appeal – and should uphold the UK's human rights obligations.

What went wrong?

The current system is failing to deliver on our principles. Child poverty rates are rising. More and more families are finding that their source of income, whether this is from work or benefits, is increasingly precarious. And, it is well documented that the benefits system can be difficult and degrading to interact with for claimants. So, where did things go wrong?

Reducing and preventing poverty

The current system fails to protect children against poverty largely because levels of support are inadequate, and because of policies which break the link between need and entitlement such as the two-child limit, the benefit cap, and the local limits on housing benefits and the 'bedroom tax'. We also need to consider whether such a heavily means-tested system is best placed to deliver on our principles. Means-tested benefits can be effective at reducing poverty; in theory, they target support at those with the greatest need. In practice, however, they are not necessarily very effective at hitting their target.

A combination of the complexity of applying for and maintaining a means-tested benefit claim, the level of intrusion involved (through the collecting of personal information), and the social control placed on claimants through the introduction of harsher conditionality, has the effect of putting some people off ever making a claim. In 2009/2010, almost a third of eligible people were not claiming a means-tested benefit that they were entitled to,[2] and estimates indicate that over £20 billion in means-tested benefits is going unclaimed.[3] One of the big promises of universal credit (UC) was that it would increase take-up. However, we have no way of confirming this as the government does not currently collect this data,[4] and one can argue that the very things that put people off claiming benefits (complexity, social control, stigma) are, if anything, worse under universal credit.

Means-tested benefits also inevitably create a poverty trap, whereby the withdrawal of benefits as earnings increase makes it hard to escape poverty through work. A lighter-touch means-testing system, with less conditionality, would be possible, and the poverty trap can be softened through the use of disregards. But in a means-tested system some degree of complexity is inevitable, and the trap cannot be completely eliminated.

Preventing poverty also means making support available for those somewhat higher up the income scale, with greater responsiveness available should needs increase. Individual entitlements are important to prevent members of couples with low or no earnings (usually women) lacking an independent income both within a household and after a couple separates. Again, both are possible in a means-tested system, but our social security system is currently moving in the other direction.

Providing income security

Income security has arguably become a more important function of the social security system, as other sources of income security for people on low incomes diminish in an increasingly insecure labour market of zero-hour contracts and weakening labour rights. However, instead of compensating for the lack of income security provided to people via the labour market, in some cases the social security system is making this income insecurity worse.

Income security is related to both the timing and reliability of income. Universal credit's strict system of monthly assessment periods is problematic here. For non-working people this creates an unnecessary five week wait for the first payment, while for workers this (and other complex rules) often mean that payments fluctuate each month due to variations in pay (or pay dates), making awards unpredictable and creating an immediate poverty trap every month.[5] Universal credit also risks claimants' security of income because it wraps a number of benefits into one. This means that claimants are highly dependent on universal credit being administered correctly, with no errors in payments and no delays, as for many claimants it may be their main or only source of income. Worryingly, however, error rates appear to be high, with one in five cases submitted to CPAG's Early Warning System[6] involving administrative error likely to result in the claimant getting the wrong amount.[7] In these situations people can be left with very little to live on, and may have to rely only on child benefit (which is straightforward to claim with no means test), or other non-means-tested benefits such as disability benefits or carer's allowance.

Many of these issues could be resolved by raising benefit levels, reducing the frequency of means testing, and allowing some level of income fluctuation before benefit payments are changed. However, means testing, through the process of income testing claimants, carries an inherent risk of errors that can have serious implications for people's lives – and these risks have been made worse through the move to 'digital by default' in universal credit.

Social solidarity

When considering the design of a future social security system, a key question must be: who is the system for? At CPAG we believe the system is for everyone, which is why we have placed social solidarity at the heart of our principles. Indeed, most adults will receive a working-age benefit at some point in their lives.[8] However, when we consider the development of social security policy over the last 20 years, it is clear that social solidarity was not in the forefront of policy makers' minds. Many aspects of the design of out-of-work benefits, and now universal credit, appear to be underpinned by a fundamental mistrust of claimants. Harsher conditionality and sanctions, the zealous clawing back of overpayments, and the minimum income floor and surplus earnings rules all help to fuel a narrative that claimants are trying to 'cheat' the system rather than being in genuine need. Instead, we need less stigma, a lighter touch and more people credited in, so more people benefit from the system and are in turn more willing to support it. We might also learn from the approach taken in Scotland, which has established its own administration for devolved benefits – Social Security Scotland. It has committed to 'putting dignity, fairness and respect at the heart of everything we do'.[9]

What should a future system look like?

We need urgent reinvestment in financial support for families to reverse the rise in child poverty. But lifting people out of poverty cannot be the *only* focus. The sole pursuit of maximising the number of people lifted above the poverty line, without considering how the system is delivered or experienced by the people who use it, will not get us very far and may even undermine the very thing it is intended to achieve. It is also not very ambitious. A reimagined social security system could do much more than reduce poverty. It could provide a decent standard of living for all children, protect us all against economic and other risks, contribute to a more equal society and treat people with dignity and respect. We also need to consider how to build public support for social security, which probably means extending its reach to more of us, not ever more targeting of those below the poverty line.

Means testing is probably here to stay in some form – neither a fully universal nor a fully contributory system look realistic in the UK today – but we need to look at rebalancing the system and reforming means testing to address its worst problems.

We would start by increasing the value of our **universal** child benefit significantly, and ending the high income child benefit tax charge. It is easy to administer, popular with the public, and has high levels of take up. Universal benefits can also help to promote social solidarity and instil public support and investment as everyone gets 'something' from the system. **Contingency-based** benefits paid to someone because of their circumstances, for example carer's allowance, offer many of the same advantages. There are very few contingency-based benefits left in the UK system, however an expansion of these benefits could help achieve all three of our principles.

A revitalised **social insurance** scheme that is inclusive in its design could also have multiple benefits, for example by providing a level of income security to higher earners (through income-related payments, which works in a number of European countries) and helping to promote social solidarity by ensuring that a wider range of people receive support from, and are therefore invested in, the social security system. Promisingly, a citizens' jury held by CPAG on the future of the social security system revealed a great deal of support for the contributory principle and for greater generosity towards those unable to work.

We must do means testing a lot better in future. Learning from the best aspects of tax credits (their predictable payments, generous disregards and the light-touch means test, which did not appear to stigmatise or distrust claimants) and from the experiences of other countries, which almost all have much less conditionality than the UK, would be a good place to start.

Conclusion

Ending child poverty for good is an ambitious task, and to make this and our principles a reality, we need a fundamental review of the current social security system. While in the short term, we need to fund universal credit adequately as well as bolstering other parts of the system, we are not too far down the universal credit road to consider alternatives. By pursuing all three of our principles in tandem we can build a system that provides a genuinely secure future for children and families.

Notes and references

1   Taken from Institute for Fiscal Studies slides, available at www.ifs.org.uk/future-of-benefits. Original source: Department for Work and Pensions, 'Benefit expenditure and caseload tables 2018'

2   D Finn and J Goodship, *Take-up of Benefits and Poverty: an evidence and policy review*, Centre for Economic and Social Inclusion, 2014

3   'Over £20 billion still unclaimed in means tested benefits', entitledto blog post, 12 December 2018, entitledto.co.uk/blog

4   G Bangham and A Corlett, 'Boosting benefit take-up is critical to the success of universal credit, but we might not be able to measure whether it's working', Resolution Foundation comment, 20 December 2018

5   J Tucker and D Norris, *Rough Justice: problems with circumstances in universal credit, and what can be done about them. Findings from CPAG's Early Warning System*, CPAG, 2018

6   CPAG's database of cases submitted by front line advisers

7   'Universal credit claimants left in the dark about their entitlements', CPAG press release, 1 May 2019

8   'IFS at 50: the future of benefits' slide presentation, February 2019, available at www.ifs.org.uk/future-of-benefits

9   See socialsecurity.gov.scot

Nineteen
Learning from Scotland?
John Dickie

1999: the start of a new era for child poverty action and for Scottish devolution

In 1999, in the same year as the then UK Prime Minister Tony Blair made the historic commitment to end child poverty within a generation, the Scottish Parliament was reconvened. Powers over policy levers such as housing, health and education (previously exercised by the Westminster government's Secretary of State for Scotland and other UK ministers), as well as limited income tax powers, were devolved. Key powers over social security, employment and economic matters remained reserved. The story of child poverty over the last 20 years, and the challenge of what needs to happen now, is therefore a story of policy making and political decisions at UK and Scotland level.

A decade of progress

At least until 2010, the child poverty story in Scotland is similar to that across the UK. Progress on an internationally and historically unprecedented scale was made. Child poverty rates in Scotland fell from 33 per cent (360,000 children) in 1996/97 to 19 per cent (190,000 children) in 2011/12.[1] This progress was achieved as a result of clear political commitment at UK and Scotland level. As elsewhere, key UK-wide interventions that improved family incomes included the introduction of the national minimum wage, increases in universal child benefit and investment in tax credits.[2] A divergent approach to social housing helped to ensure housing costs, and the subsequent risk of poverty (as measured after housing costs), were lower relative to the rest of the UK, supporting faster progress on child poverty in Scotland.[3] Devolved policy on employability and childcare including, for example, the Working for Families programme which supported parents toward employment by removing childcare barriers, as well as investment in welfare rights advice and a limited extension of free school meal entitlement, helped support these key UK-wide policies to increase family resources.

As at UK level, the focus of Scottish anti-poverty policy was to support parents into work. Following on from the Labour/Liberal Democrat coalition's anti-poverty strategy,[4] the SNP government from 2007 set out a joint framework with local authorities for tackling poverty,[5] including key commitments to making work pay. Nevertheless, low pay, job insecurity, lack of flexibility for working parents and sparse in-work support for those with a disability or long-term illness continued to undermine work as a route out of poverty, with an increasing proportion of children in poverty living in working families.[6]

In 2010, the UK Child Poverty Act placed a duty on the Scottish government to produce strategies setting out the measures it would take to contribute towards child poverty targets. The subsequent strategies (2011 and 2014) were welcomed as identifying the range of devolved policy areas where action could be taken to reduce and prevent poverty. However, arguably the strategies were never accompanied by a clear enough delivery plan, and there was not a clear link with national or local budget setting. Nevertheless, Scottish policy was making a real difference to low-income families, albeit not on a scale to affect overall child poverty trends. Free school meals were extended to all children in the first three years of primary school, and divergent approaches taken as elements of UK social security were abolished. In 2013, the Scottish Welfare Fund was established to replace the UK social fund with increased investment, a statutory underpinning and a replacement of crisis loans with grants. Following the abolition of council tax benefit, a new council tax reduction scheme protected the level of support with council tax available to families, and action was taken to, in effect, abolish the UK government's 'bedroom tax' through use of discretionary housing payments.

Rising child poverty...

Despite these distinct Scottish policies, extraordinary cuts to UK social security have, just as elsewhere in the UK, led to significant increases in child poverty. By 2020/21 an estimated £3.7 billion a year of social security support will have been lost in Scotland as a result of UK-wide cuts, with families, in and out of work, bearing the bulk of this loss.[7] These cuts are the key driver of rising child poverty with almost one in four (240,000) of

Scotland's children again officially living in poverty. Worse still, in the absence of significant policy change, this figure will increase dramatically. Scottish government forecasts indicate it will reach 38 per cent by 2030/31,[8] while Resolution Foundation analysis suggests a child poverty rate of 29 per cent by 2023/24 – the highest in over 20 years,[9] reversing the progress made since the 1990s.[10]

... but room for some optimism – the Child Poverty (Scotland) Act and new 2030 targets

Despite this gloomy context, and the damage that is being wreaked on the lives of an increasing number of children, there is room for some optimism. In 2017, following significant influencing work by CPAG and others, the Scottish Parliament unanimously passed the Child Poverty (Scotland) Act. The Act set targets to reduce child poverty by 2030 – largely replicating the now scrapped UK 2020 targets but using the arguably more ambitious after housing costs measure of low income that more accurately reflects what families have to live on. In addition, the Scottish government must produce delivery plans setting out how these targets will be met, and report annually on progress. The first delivery plan (2018–2022)[11] was welcomed by CPAG and others as setting out in the clearest terms yet an understanding of the key drivers of child poverty – income from employment, income from social security and the costs of living – and identifying the right areas of action to address these drivers. However, there is real concern that it is not yet clear what scale of impact actions set out in the plan (for example, on income maximisation, parental employment and housing) are expected to have, whether they are sufficient to make substantive progress against the targets, and crucially what resources will be needed. It is not yet clear how the Scottish budget process is prioritising child poverty to the extent needed to deliver against the targets.[12]

Real investment in financial support for families

Nevertheless, real investment is being made, including in the use of new social security powers.[13] The £500 Sure Start grant provided elsewhere in the UK has been replaced with Best Start grants for low-income families, with a £600 pregnancy and baby payment for the first child (£300 for second and subsequent children) and two new early years and school-age payments of £250, again for children in lower income families as they reach nursery and then primary school age. While not in themselves sufficient to make an impact on overall rates of child poverty, they provide low-income families with very real additional support. A minimum £100 school clothing grant for children in low-income families has also been introduced, and there is real focus on building income maximisation into mainstream services.[14] Early learning and childcare is also being expanded, with 1140 hours of free provision[15] to be available from August 2020, potentially reducing the costs of childcare and removing barriers to work.

The Child Poverty (Scotland) Act 2017 also created, for the first time, a duty on local authorities and NHS boards to produce joint annual local child poverty action reports. Guidance[16] setting out expectations of the reports suggest they should articulate a 'step change' in the priority attached to tackling child poverty at local level. With the first year of reports published, there is evidence of increased focus, innovation and enthusiasm for tackling child poverty at local level,[17] although there is more to be done to ensure all local policy levers are used to maximum effect. The reporting duty creates an opportunity to bring in new actors previously less focused on child poverty, including from economic development and transport – and there is evidence of this beginning to happen.

The new Scottish child payment – a game-changer?

Despite these positive developments, recent projections highlight that Scotland is nowhere near on target to reach its child poverty goals.[18] That is why the Scottish government announcement of a Scottish child payment, following several years of campaigning led by CPAG, is so important. The new payment of an additional £10 per week for each child in families in receipt of universal credit[19] is to be introduced for under-six's by Christmas 2020, and for all eligible children under 16 before the end of 2022. It is estimated it will lift up to 30,000 children out of poverty, a three-percentage point reduction by 2023/24.[20] This commitment is a game-changer in using devolved social security powers to directly tackle poverty, with potential to substantively alter the current upward trend.

More needed to meet 2030 targets

The harsh reality, however, is that even this investment, modelled to lift 30,000 children from poverty, is counterbalanced by cuts to the value of UK social security that look set to increase child poverty by 50,000 by 2023.[21] To reach the 2030 targets will require a reduction in child poverty of 140,000. Even to make any progress against these targets needs a doubling of the value of the new child payment.

Of course, social security alone cannot end poverty. Efforts must continue to improve income from employment and to reduce the childcare, housing, energy, transport and education costs that lock too many families in poverty. The new UK government needs to work with Scottish and local government, act to restore the value of children's benefits and make ending child poverty a UK as well as a Scottish priority. However, if Scotland is serious about meeting the 2030 targets, and ending poverty in all its forms, the Scottish parliament will need to build on the Scottish child payment and plan strategically how its value and impact can be increased in the coming years.

Notes and references

1   https://www.gov.scot/publications/poverty-income-inequality-scotland-2015-18
2   R Joyce, *Child Poverty in Britain: recent trends and future prospects*, IFS Working Paper W15/07, Institute for Fiscal Studies, 2015
3   E Congreve, *Poverty in Scotland 2019*, Joseph Rowntree Foundation, 2019
4   JH McKendrick and others, *Closing the Opportunity Gap Programme: Phase 1 evaluation*, Scottish Government, 2007
5   Scottish Government, *Achieving Our Potential: a framework to tackle poverty and income inequality in Scotland*, 2008
6   Up from 49 per cent in 2007–10 to 65 per cent in 2015–18. See *Poverty and Income Inequality in Scotland: 2015–18*, Scottish Government, March 2019, p4
7   Scottish Government, *Welfare Reform: annual report 2019*, September 2019, p13
8   H Reed and G Stark, *Forecasting Child Poverty in Scotland*, Scottish Government, 2018, Chapter 1
9   A Corlett, *Wrong Direction: can Scotland hit its child poverty targets?*, Resolution Foundation, 2019
10 A Hood and T Waters, *Living Standards, Poverty and Inequality in the UK: 2017–18 to 2021–22*, Institute for Fiscal Studies, 2017
11 Scottish Government, *Every Child, Every Chance: the Tackling Child Poverty Delivery Plan 2018–22*, March 2018
12 See, for example, Poverty and Inequality Commission, *Poverty and Inequality Commission's Response to the Scottish Budget 2019–20*, May 2019; and Joseph Rowntree Foundation and Fraser of Allander Institute blog, 'How does the Scottish Government assess the impact of its budget on tackling child poverty?', 10 January 2019,

https://fraserofallander.org

13 Devolved under the Scotland Act 2016.

14 For example, through the Healthier, Wealthier Children programme, creating referral pathways between health services and welfare advice services, gcph.co.uk/children_and_families/family_and_child_poverty/healthier_wealthier_children.

15 Up from current 600 hours. See Scottish government, 'Early learning and childcare expansion', gov.scot/policies/early-education-and-care/early-learning-and-childcare.

16 Scottish Government, *Developing a Local Child Poverty Action Report: guidance*, 2018

17 As the Poverty and Inequality Commission has reflected in *Poverty and Inequality Commission's Review of the Local Child Poverty Action Reports 2019*, November 2019.

18 A Corlett, *Wrong Direction: can Scotland hit its child poverty targets?*, Resolution Foundation, 2019

19 Or equivalent legacy benefits.

20 Scottish Government, 'Scottish Child Payment', gov.scot/policies/social-security/scottish-child-payment

21 R Gunson, '"People can't wait" – when could Scotland's new Income Supplement be introduced?', IPPR Scotland blog post, Institute for Public Policy Research, 24 May 2019

Twenty

A new child poverty strategy: ending it for good[1]

Lizzie Flew

The last Labour government set out an ambitious agenda following Tony Blair's 1999 pledge to end child poverty. The strategy focused on: work, through policies including the New Deal for Lone Parents and the minimum wage; financial support in the form of tax credits, increases to child benefit and help with childcare costs; and investment in services such as Sure Start. At the same time, ambitious efforts were made to bring down health inequalities, and to promote inclusive education and children's services under the 'Every Child Matters' agenda. The drive to eradicate child poverty spanned all departments, led by the Treasury, and child poverty fell.

Cross-party agreement was reached on the need to tackle child poverty by the time of the 2010 election, resulting in the Child Poverty Act 2010. The Act set out child poverty reduction targets and created a duty for the government to introduce, and report against, a child poverty strategy, which was to cover:

- skills and employment of parents;

- financial support for children and parents;

- information, advice and assistance to parents and the promotion of parenting skills;

- physical and mental health, education, childcare and social services;

- housing, the built or natural environment and the promotion of social inclusion.

However, the Coalition government's two child poverty strategies did not sufficiently address families' material resources and the high costs they faced, and child poverty started to rise. The first strategy, *A New Approach to Child Poverty: tackling the causes of disadvantage and transforming families' lives*, focussed on 'combating worklessness and educational failure and preventing family and relationship breakdown', rather than family incomes.

Not only that, but over the course of the strategy, the government began the introduction of cuts to social security, including cuts to tax credits, housing benefit and council tax support, the introduction of the 'bedroom tax' and benefit cap, the move from Disability Living Allowance to Personal Independence Payment, reduced value and shorter entitlement periods for contributory benefits and the abolition of the social fund (replaced in England by non-ring-fenced local welfare assistance schemes, and in Scotland and Wales by new devolved schemes). Many benefits were also uprated below inflation. And services were heavily cut, with the loss of hundreds of Sure Start centres, for example.

The second strategy, *Child Poverty Strategy 2014–17*, included rhetoric on tackling child poverty:

> Whilst some children thrive despite the poverty they grow up in, for many children growing up in poverty can mean a childhood of insecurity, underachievement at school, poor health and isolation from their peers.

But this period saw the announcement of further enormous cuts to social security, including the four-year benefit freeze, lower benefit cap and the two-child limit. In 2017, the Welfare Reform and Work Act 2016 renamed the Child Poverty Act the Life Chances Act, and removed the requirement for a child poverty strategy. A long-promised 'life chances strategy' never materialised, and instead the government published *Improving Lives: helping workless families*. Given we know that most children in poverty live in working families, and that the prevalence of long-term worklessness and its effects on child outcomes have been greatly overstated,[2] this was hardly an appropriate replacement. Since then, there has been no evidence of a policy focus on tackling child poverty, which has continued to rise.

What do we do next?

It is clear that with leadership, ambition and effective policy-making we can reduce child poverty. A child poverty strategy needs to take a **wide, co-ordinated and long-term** approach, investing to reduce poverty now, but also to **prevent** poverty. It needs to be **integrated with other strategies**, and based on the **best interests of the child**. It needs to take into account **children's rights**, and therefore be informed by children and their parents. It needs to focus on **children at risk**, including children in lone-parent families, larger families and young families; disadvantaged regions of the UK; families where someone has a disability; Traveller and Roma children; children from black and minority ethnic backgrounds; children in care; homeless children; and refugee children. And it needs to **balance universal and targeted support**, so all children can benefit from a common universal platform of support, with additional help for those who need it. A UK-wide child poverty strategy should have seven key components.

1 Clear leadership, infrastructure and targets to work towards

The government needs to commit to ending child poverty, set an ambitious target, such as 15 years with interim targets along the way, and back this with adequate resources. Commitment and leadership must be echoed by devolved administrations and local authorities in their child poverty strategies, backed by adequate resources. To ensure long-term success, the government must make the case and build lasting public support for ending child poverty.

To measure progress, we need to monitor (both before and after housing costs):

- relative low income;

- combined low income and material deprivation;

- anchored (absolute) low income;

- persistent poverty;

- poverty depth.

To ensure the child poverty strategy is embraced by all departments we need a dedicated team in 10 Downing Street. All policy proposals and decisions which have a bearing on children and families should contain an impact assessment on children's rights, child wellbeing and child poverty. The current family test has proven completely inadequate in preventing policies which have a very detrimental impact on family life from being introduced. We need a Child Poverty Commission which provides advice and research, and holds the government to account on the targets, and for the UN Convention on the Rights of the Child to be incorporated into UK law.

2 Social security that supports us all

Social security should be strengthened to ensure it is there for all of us when we need it, and that it meets the following core principles (see Chapter 18).

- It should prevent and reduce poverty, by providing an adequate income and support with additional costs (such as for people with disabilities and for parents), supporting paid and unpaid work, and protecting people against economic uncertainty.

- It should provide income security, by responding to life events (such as having a child or becoming unwell) as well as providing a minimum level of income security at *all* times.

- It should promote social solidarity and social integration, support individual autonomy, reduce inequalities and enjoy public trust and support.

Its delivery should: treat people with dignity and respect; be simple for users and flexible enough to respond to individual needs; promote individual autonomy; be based on human rights and a clear legal framework for entitlements; maximise take-up with support for vulnerable claimants and a right to advice; and provide mechanisms for user voices to be heard. As an immediate step, we need to raise the level of support for children and families in the current system by restoring the value lost from working-age benefits due to the four-year freeze; adding £5 a week to child benefit and removing the high income tax charge; scrapping the 'bedroom tax', benefit cap and two-child limit; increasing work incentives in universal credit including for second earners; and greatly reducing the use of sanctions. All families should be able to access welfare rights advice.

3 Decent work, pay and progression

Because the labour market does not always help families move out of poverty, the strategy needs to focus on the world of work. Paid work will sometimes not pay well enough, and some jobs offer insufficient or precarious hours. Caring for family members is unpaid. Lone-parent families are often in poverty despite being in work because they are combining low-paid and under-valued employment with caring for children. In couples, it is often the absence of a 'second earner' that affects whether that family is in poverty.

Wages cannot account for family size, so the government's child poverty strategy must include action on the social security system as above (see Chapter 18) but also on:

- wage levels, raising the minimum wage to the level of the real living wage for all workers;

- contracts, so that workers benefit from greater job security and more predictable hours and shifts, for example following the standards set by the Living Hours Standard;[3]

- flexible, family-friendly working;

- the gender pay gap (see also the section below on childcare);

- employment and progression opportunities for 'second earners';

- maternity, paternity and parental leave provisions;

- employment support which is provided outside of any benefit conditionality regime;

- childcare so that parents can work the hours which work for their family.

4 Quality, affordable childcare when families need it

The child poverty strategy needs to include a comprehensive, universal childcare offer for families that is high quality, affordable and available when families need it. Not only does this help parents work, but it also ensures that younger children get the benefit of early years education, and school-age children can benefit from enriching extra-curricular activities and holiday clubs.

Special attention needs to be paid to childcare for the following groups, where provision is currently woefully inadequate:

- those working outside the 9 to 5 pattern;

- children with special educational needs and disabilities;

- school-age children before and after the school day and in the holidays.

A universal programme of high-quality pre-school childcare and extended school hours, including enriching activities and food, would benefit children, promote inclusion by removing stigmas associated with targeted programmes (such as 'holiday hunger' schemes) and allow parents greater flexibility in their working choices.

5 Inclusive education

Poverty can affect children's learning. The child poverty strategy needs to address costs within school as well as support for children living in poverty. In particular it should focus on:

* the pupil premium and funding for schools in disadvantaged communities;

* implementing universal free school meals;

* efforts to minimise the costs of participation – for example, uniforms, equipment and trips;

* encouraging school facilities to be deployed for the benefit of whole communities through, for example, holiday clubs and adult learning;

* an asset-based, rather than deficit-based, approach to education (see Chapter 14).

6 Secure homes for families

A safe, warm and secure home, together with a healthy environment, provide the foundation for a decent childhood and good educational attainment. Children need space to do homework and safe outdoor places in which to play. Initially, a child poverty strategy needs to ensure that housing support covers actual rents. Then there is an urgent need to build genuinely affordable rented homes and social housing (see Chapter 16). The strategy should also address:

* the quality and safety of rented homes;

* more protections for renters and longer tenancies;

* availability of suitable housing for children with disabilities and long-term health conditions;

* temporary accommodation;

* energy efficiency to reduce fuel costs;

- affordable local amenities such as public transport, parks, sports grounds, leisure facilities, youth centres and libraries;

- road safety and air pollution on routes commonly used by children (e.g. around schools).

7 Services and support

In addition to material assistance, parents need information, advice and support. A child poverty strategy should provide for universal parenting support. Support provided through high-quality children's centres would offer valuable help for development and learning at home (see Chapter 12). A child poverty strategy also needs to be connected to universal high-quality health and social care and youth services, to ensure that all children – regardless of their economic circumstances – can be supported to enjoy good health and wellbeing and reach their full potential.

Conclusion

By addressing families' material resources, not only can children get a healthy diet, toys and books, and school trips, but also the stress and anxiety experienced by parents and children when there are money worries disappear – as does the sense of exclusion and shame which children may experience when they are unable to join in sports or music activities with their friends, or when they are bullied for being poor. By addressing childcare, housing, education and parenting support, a child poverty strategy can ensure children have enriching childhood experiences and good life chances. Enshrining these initiatives in a strategy with cross-party support, statutory targets and meaningful leadership will ensure its long-term success.

But not only does the child poverty strategy need to be comprehensive, it needs to form part of a wider focus on children – their childhoods and their futures. For example, a child poverty strategy should link into a children's health strategy because reducing poverty would improve children's mental and physical health. It is through this sustained, co-ordinated effort, with all parts of government pulling in the same direction, that we can end child poverty for good.

Notes and references

1   This chapter draws on a longer paper on what a child poverty strategy should look like written by Jonathan Bradshaw, Fran Bennett, Alison Garnham, Imran Hussain and Ruth Lister.

2   J Bradshaw, O Movshuk and G Rees, 'It's poverty, not worklessness', *Poverty*, 158, autumn 2017

3   *Living Hours: providing security of hours alongside a real Living Wage*, Living Wage Foundation, 2019

Twenty-one

Child poverty reduction in New Zealand

Jacinda Ardern and Kristie Carter

Foreword by Jacinda Ardern

A country with the relative abundance of New Zealand can and should be the best place in the world to be a child. While in global terms, most young New Zealanders are doing well, the reality is that many are not experiencing anything close to a good life. Improving the standard of living for children in my country is the reason I entered politics, and why my Government has committed to halving child poverty within a decade.

As the first step, our Parliament passed legislation, with cross-party support, that encourages a focus on child wellbeing and poverty reduction, and ensures that Governments now – and in the future – are held to account for decisions that have economic, fiscal and wellbeing impacts on children living in poverty. The Child Poverty Reduction Act 2018 recognises we must have an enduring commitment in this area if we are to see long-term systemic change. The approach we take to our Wellbeing Budget places a unique focus on addressing child poverty by targeting its symptoms and causes, because it's the right thing to do for our communities and our economy.

Measuring poverty is one thing; setting goals to reduce it is another, but making sure that we have an action plan that captures the voices of children is critical. That is why New Zealand has further adopted a Child and Youth Wellbeing Strategy.

Shaped by the voices and views of more than 6,000 children and young people, during its development I received over 1,000 postcards from children and young people. I read every one. The messages were clear: children are concerned about everything from mental health and the wellbeing of their peers, to whether or not their peers have enough food to eat, enough money in the household to thrive, to participate, to feel like they're making the most of their talents and their opportunities.

These actions are the first steps in a journey to greater prosperity and outcomes for our children – a shared journey that will require the collective efforts of community groups, ongoing partnerships with business and Māori, as we simply cannot achieve this on our own. That is the challenge, and the call to action to meet our vision that New Zealand is the best place in the world for children and young people.

Rt Hon Jacinda Ardern
Prime Minister of New Zealand
Minister for Child Poverty Reduction

The nature and scale of the problem in New Zealand

While most young New Zealanders experience good wellbeing, too many children and young people and their families are facing significant, often ongoing, adversity, deprivation and stress which reduces their wellbeing and life opportunities.

In the New Zealand context, poverty has been defined as the exclusion from a minimum acceptable standard of living because of a lack of adequate resources. It is primarily about a family's available resources not meeting their basic material needs, and it is estimated there were between 150,000 and 250,000 children living in poverty in 2017/18.

Evidence shows that the experience of poverty, especially when it is severe and persistent, can have a negative impact on the lives of children – on average, they are more likely to experience poorer educational outcomes, poorer health, and have more difficulty finding work in adulthood. The harmful effects can last into adulthood and impact on society as a whole.

The current government brought a focus to child poverty reduction and child wellbeing through legislation. Soon after coming into office in 2017, the government set a vision that New Zealand be the best place in the world for children and young people. As the first step, the Prime Minister, Rt Hon Jacinda Ardern, as the Minister for Child Poverty Reduction, introduced legislation to ensure ongoing political accountability for reducing child poverty and improving child wellbeing. This significant legislation was passed into law on 20 December 2018 with near unanimous parliamentary support. The Child Poverty Reduction Bill (which was divided into two bills at its final reading) became the Child Poverty Reduction Act 2018 and the Children's Amendment Act 2018,[1] helping to ensure enduring commitment to reducing child poverty and improving child wellbeing.

The Child Poverty Reduction Act and its main provisions

The Child Poverty Reduction Act 2018 requires the government of the day to:

- set long-term (10-year) and intermediate (three-year) targets on the defined set of child poverty primary measures;

- report annually on the set of child poverty measures, four primary and six secondary measures. New Zealand's statistics agency Stats NZ is responsible for annual reporting on child poverty rates and these measure child poverty at different depths;

- report each Budget day on how investment in the Budget will reduce child poverty and how the government is progressing towards its child poverty reduction targets;

- report on child poverty-related indicators (CPRIs), measures of a cause, consequence or correlate of child poverty. The CPRIs identified by the Minister are: housing affordability, housing quality, food insecurity, regular school attendance and avoidable hospitalisations.

Amendments to the Children's Act (2014) require successive governments to develop and publish a strategy to improve the wellbeing of all children and young people, with a particular focus on child poverty and those with greater needs.

Child poverty measures and targets

The legislation establishes a balanced suite of measures to measure and report on child poverty. They will allow us to track progress towards the targets, allow some international comparison, and provide a good picture of the impact of policy decisions on the lives of children.

The Act requires the Minister for Child Poverty Reduction (currently the Prime Minister Rt Hon Jacinda Ardern) to set three-year (intermediate) and 10-year (long-term) targets for the reduction of child poverty rates. The targets are aligned with the sustainable development goal of reducing poverty by at least half by 2030 and have been described as ambitious by domestic observers. Targets have been set for three 'primary' measures of child poverty, as outlined in Table 21.1.

Table 21.1:
Targets for three primary child poverty measures

Primary measure	Baseline rate (2017/18)	3-year target rate (2020/21)	10-year target rate (2027/28)
Proportion of children in households with **low income** (below 50 per cent of median income) **before deducting housing costs**, using a **moving line**/relative measure	16%	10%	5%
Proportion of children in households with **low income** (below 50 per cent of median income) **after deducting housing costs**, using a **fixed line** measure (set at 2017/18)	23%	19%	10%
Proportion of children in households facing **material hardship** (defined as a lack of six or more items out of 17: going without things such as healthy food, suitable clothes, or delaying going to the doctor)	13%	10%	6%

Targets must also be set for the proportion of children in households facing persistent poverty by 2024. Persistent poverty generally measures those facing poverty over multiple years. Stats NZ is currently developing this measure.

Budget day reporting and impacts on child poverty

The Child Poverty Reduction Act 2018 requires that as part of the Budget day reporting, the government must report on progress toward the targets, and how the Budget will affect child poverty, both positively and negatively. The first Budget 2019 report is available at budget.govt.nz/budget/2019/wellbeing/child-poverty-report/index.htm.[2]

Reducing child poverty and improving child wellbeing is prioritised as an area for investment, reflecting the government's commitment. This government has already implemented a number of policies to reduce child poverty and make progress towards its targets. Some of the initiatives that have already been implemented are designed to directly impact children living in poverty by putting more money in the pockets of parents, while others are more indirect and designed to ease the pressures faced by families, such as changes to health, housing and education settings.

Some examples of recent initiatives focussed on child poverty reduction include:

- Families Package: $5.5 billion over four years – increasing the Family Tax Credit; Accommodation Supplement; and introducing the Winter Energy Payment and Best Start child payment

- indexing main benefits to average wage growth

- improving the affordability and availability of housing

- extending paid parental leave

- expanding health services to children in disadvantaged schools and children under the age of 14 years

- reducing school costs for families

- prototyping a free school lunch programme in disadvantaged schools

- increased investment in data to measure child poverty.

The Child and Youth Wellbeing Strategy

As part of the Child Poverty Reduction legislation, amendments were made to the Children's Act 2014 (enacted in 2018) which sets out specific requirements for the government of the day to develop and publish a child wellbeing strategy, with a particular focus on child poverty and those with greater needs.

New Zealand's first Child and Youth Wellbeing Strategy[3] was launched in August 2019. The Strategy sets out a shared understanding of what is important for child and youth wellbeing across multiple domains, what the government is doing, and how others can help. The Strategy draws on the best evidence from social science and cultural wellbeing frameworks. For the Strategy to best reflect what is important to New Zealanders and, more importantly, children, it was developed with input from 10,000 New Zealanders – including over 6,000 children and young people, who told us what makes for a good life, what gets in the way, and what we should do about it. Some key insights we learned from young people are:

- 'Accept us for who we are and who we want to be.'
- 'Life is really hard for some of us.'
- 'We all deserve more than just the basics.'
- 'To help us, help our whānau/family and our support crew.'

The Strategy includes a Programme of Action that sets out the policies, programmes and plans to achieve the vision and outcomes. The current Programme of Action (75 actions and 49 supporting actions, led by 20 government agencies) reflects the strong call from children and New Zealanders to urgently reduce the current inequity of outcomes.

The legislation underpinning the Strategy ensures transparency and accountability through annual reporting of outcomes. An initial set of 36 indicators and corresponding measures has been established, to help measure progress and identify where more work might be needed. The Strategy is also required to be reviewed at least every three years, to ensure it continues to address the issues and challenges facing New Zealand's children and young people.

Many of the issues facing children, young people and their families are complex, stubborn and intergenerational, so change will take time. It will also require a unified response, and the Strategy seeks to support, encourage and mobilise action by others, and empower and enable people and communities to drive the solutions that work for them.

Find out more at: https://childyouthwellbeing.govt.nz.

Notes and references

1 Department of the Prime Minister and Cabinet, New Zealand, 'Child poverty reduction and wellbeing legislation', https://dpmc.govt.nz/our-programmes/reducing-child-poverty/child-poverty-reduction-and-wellbeing-legislation

2 https://www.budget.govt.nz/budget/2019/wellbeing/child-poverty-report/index.htm

3 https://childyouthwellbeing.govt.nz/resources/child-and-youth-wellbeing-strategy